NEW DIRECTIONS FOR INSTITUTIONAL RESEARCH

Patrick T. Terenzini
The Pennsylvania State University
EDITOR-IN-CHIEF

Ellen Earle Chaffee
North Dakota University System
ASSOCIATE EDITOR

Managing with Scarce Resources

William B. Simpson
California State University, Los Angeles

EDITOR

D0167593

Number 79, Fall 1993

JOSSEY-BASS PUBLISHERS
San Francisco

MANAGING WITH SCARCE RESOURCES
William B. Simpson (ed.)
New Directions for Institutional Research, no. 79
Volume XV, Number 3
Patrick T. Terenzini, Editor-in-Chief
Ellen Earle Chaffee, Associate Editor

Microfilm copies of issues and articles are available in 16mm and 35mm, as well as microfiche in 105mm, through University Microfilms Inc., 300 North Zeeb Road, Ann Arbor, Michigan 48106-1346.

LC 85-645339   ISSN 0271-0579   ISBN 1-55542-724-3

NEW DIRECTIONS FOR INSTITUTIONAL RESEARCH is part of The Jossey-Bass Higher and Adult Education Series and is published quarterly by Jossey-Bass Inc., Publishers, 350 Sansome Street, San Francisco, California 94104-1342 (publication number USPS 098-830). Second-class postage paid at San Francisco, California, and at additional mailing offices. POST-MASTER: Send address changes to New Directions for Institutional Research, Jossey-Bass Inc., Publishers, 350 Sansome Street, San Francisco, California 94104-1342.

SUBSCRIPTIONS for 1993 cost $45.00 for individuals and $60.00 for institutions, agencies, and libraries.

EDITORIAL CORRESPONDENCE should be sent to the editor-in-chief, Patrick T. Terenzini, Center for the Study of Higher Education, The Pennsylvania State University, 403 South Allen Street, Suite 104, University Park, Pennsylvania 16801-5202.

Photograph of the library by Michael Graves at San Juan Capistrano by Chad Slattery © 1984. All rights reserved.

Manufactured in the United States of America. Nearly all Jossey-Bass books, jackets, and periodicals are printed on recycled paper that contains at least 50 percent recycled waste, including 10 percent postconsumer waste. Many of our materials are also printed with vegetable-based ink; during the printing process these inks emit fewer volatile organic compounds (VOCs) than petroleum-based inks. VOCs contribute to the formation of smog.

CONTENTS

EDITOR'S NOTES

Managing with scarce resources in an enterprise like higher education refers in its broadest sense to the stewardship role that we must play when we use resources, the total availability of which is limited at any given time and which accordingly have to be diverted from alternative uses, including uses such as improving the quality of life in the inner city and protecting the environment. Two considerations justify this diversion: Higher education directly and indirectly increases the effectiveness of the human component of our resources, and increasing the effectiveness of the human component leads in the long run to an increase in the resources available.

In addition to demographic trends, the demand for higher education reflects several concurrent developments: the increase in the complexity of life for which education prepares individuals; the increased recognition by individuals, employers, and government of the extent of education needed; and the increased access made possible for underrepresented elements of our population.

However, the term *scarcity* in this volume reflects two other perspectives: First, resources in higher education are not adequate to provide education to all who seek it at the level of quality and levels of tuition and other requirements in effect. Second, these resources are even less adequate if we wish to implement fully the higher education objectives to which public policy subscribes.

Consider the hypothetical condition under which there would be no scarcity from the first perspective. If postsecondary education in a particular field were a standardized product with multiple providers in a single market and if there were no inhibitions as to limiting access, then a price (tuition and other requirements) would emerge through the operation of impersonal market forces so as to bring the quantity of education financed and supplied at that price equal to the demand for enrollment from those who could afford that price. While resources would not be scarce under these conditions from the first perspective, there would most certainly still be a shortfall from the second perspective. That is, we would still not achieve various policy goals, including those relating to equal opportunity and to the importance of having an educated work force and citizenry.

Taking into account that prospective students differentiate among the offerings of competing institutions and that one institution can therefore raise tuition without driving all applicants to an institution with a lower price, we recognize that price is determined not by impersonal market forces but instead by administrators in accord with the goals and needs of their institution.

If a postsecondary institution sought to maximize profit by equating changes in cost and revenue at the margin and if it were profitable in this

enterprise, it would serve fewer students than it would have if it had elected instead simply to break even in terms of average cost and average revenue.

The contributions to this volume focus on not-for-profit colleges and universities—institutions that emphatically do not regard higher education simply as a product to be bought in the marketplace by those who can afford it. Nonprofit institutions set price lower than institutions for profit in order to increase the number of students who can attend. (There are two exceptions: The institution may raise tuition in search of status or in order to finance its student financial aid program.) To the extent an institution holds tuition and fees below the level at which it covers its own costs, it has to finance the difference through endowment earnings, reserve funds, alumni contributions, foundation or other grants, and, especially for public institutions, appropriations from various levels of government. This volume discusses how an institution can respond to, or seek to prevent, a shortfall in resources relative to costs.

In Chapter One, William H. Pickens reviews the extent to which state and federal appropriations have kept pace with enrollment and inflation. He then sets forth principles as to how an individual institution can use cross-sectional comparisons to evaluate the adequacy of its resources to the task of providing education at an acceptable level of quality to individuals seeking it at the levels of tuition and other requirements currently in effect. He articulates these principles as a series of steps.

Subsequent chapters deal with the ways in which an institution of higher education can best respond to resource scarcity. Contributors emphasize options available to a single campus or a system or consortium of higher education institutions over options that require broad-based efforts to change public views or national policy. Moreover, we pay attention primarily to cost containment and cost reduction rather than to the revenue side of the problem. More on these topics and on the areas not covered in this volume can be found in Simpson (1991), a publication that covers cost containment strategies for public policy as well as for institutional administration.

In Chapter Two, I identify significant options available to institutions that are primarily instructional. In Chapter Three, William C. Norris and Geraldine MacDonald evaluate the increased use of new technology in instruction and in administration, respectively. In Chapter Four, Joseph Froomkin concentrates on the difficult choices that research universities now face.

In Chapter Five, Stefan D. Bloomfield discusses how to organize the process of developing the options to be considered in dealing with resource scarcity. In Chapter Six, Judith M. Gappa discusses participation in the actual decisions. The expression *managing with* in the title of this volume refers to coping, not to management with a capital M. Thus, Gappa explains the sharing of decision making among and the division of decision making between faculty, administration, and academic unions where they are present. In Chapter Seven, I identify the challenges that lie ahead.

Finally, I wish to acknowledge the assistance of Ruth Decker Simpson throughout the preparation of this publication. I also thank Ellen Earle Chaffee, associate editor of this series, for her assistance.

William B. Simpson
Editor

Reference

Simpson, W. B. *Cost Containment for Higher Education: Strategies for Public Policy and Institutional Administration.* New York: Praeger, 1991.

WILLIAM B. SIMPSON is emeritus professor of economics at California State University, Los Angeles, and formerly was managing editor and coeditor of Econometrica *and executive director of the Cowles Commission for Research in Economics at the University of Chicago.*

An overview of resources for higher education over the past forty years, with special emphasis on the abundance of the 1980s and the crisis of the 1990s, this chapter pays attention to trends in government support and to ways in which individual institutions can measure the adequacy of their resources for the pursuit of their policy goals.

Measures of Resource Scarcity in Higher Education

William H. Pickens

How ironic that the very success and prominence of higher education now make it so vulnerable. Even critics of American higher education take note of its long-term growth from an enterprise utilizing less than 0.6 percent of the nation's gross national product in 1929 to the $171.6 billion, or 2.7 percent of gross national product, that it absorbed in 1992 (U.S. Department of Education, 1992).

Growth was especially impressive between 1961 and 1987, when inflation-adjusted dollar expenditures per full-time-equivalent student (FTES) in the public sector increased by 41 percent to $6,329—a 1.3 percent annual rate. For private institutions, the growth was 68 percent to $9,328, a 2 percent annual rate (Halstead, 1991). As the 1980s ended, the whole enterprise appeared robust to outsiders, flush with dollars and prestige.

The mood is different now and much more grim. Now, the prognosis is almost universal that there will be a prolonged period of limited resources. Everywhere we hear that resources are scarce.

Higher education now serves more students than ever. Enrollments have quadrupled since 1950, up to 14.3 million students in 1992. The numbers have grown even in periods when projections based on declines in the number of eighteen- to twenty-four-year-olds indicated sharp declines. Over the decades, the growth represented a singular expansion of access. An increasing proportion of eighteen- to twenty-four-year-olds attended college, especially women, and increasingly large numbers of older adults enrolled for credit.

Higher education is a much different enterprise now than it was a generation ago. Colleges and universities have grown not just in size but

NEW DIRECTIONS FOR INSTITUTIONAL RESEARCH, no. 79, Fall 1993   © Jossey-Bass Publishers

dramatically in scope, diversity, and responsibilities. The mixture of expenditures has shifted, demands have changed, the clientele has become more diverse, and technology has shaped its operation in profound ways. Resources are scarce because higher education does not have the financial support to fulfill all the commitments that it has made and all the expectations that it has raised.

Long-Term Trends in Expenditures

The 1950s and 1960s were decades when "the nation poured vast sums of new money into higher education" (Bowen, 1980, p. 29). When expenditures per FTES for support and capital outlay are deflated for price level changes, they increased by 3.5 percent per year (Bowen, 1980). Halstead's (1991) data show a slightly lower (but still substantial) annual increase for the 1960s because his inflation measure is more sophisticated and because he focuses on educational and general expenditures. One major reason for this growth was that faculty salaries outpaced the CPI by a cumulative 28 percent between 1960 and 1970 (Frances, 1992). Research and contract work grew even faster than other expenditure items, even during periods when enrollments were expanding (Froomkin, 1990). In addition to recognizing higher education's role in promoting national security, Americans invested in expanding opportunities and promoting social mobility, with increased expenditures for remedial education and special programs for disadvantaged students (Brinkman, 1990). "Funds were sufficient," Bowen (1980, p. 32) concluded, "to allow increases in real wages and salaries at a rate even faster than that in the technologically more progressive industries and at the same time to allow increased enrollment, expanded research, and improved quality."

A second phase began during the early 1970s, when the growth of revenue slowed dramatically; indeed, in several years, it actually declined. This phase was caused in part by a slowdown in the growth of enrollment and in part by a surplus of candidates for the professoriate (Cheit, 1973; Cartter, 1976). Bowen (1980) calculated a 2.3 percent loss per FTES for all higher education in the 1970s, while Halstead (1991) documented an anemic 0.67 percent rise for public institutions between 1974 and 1982 and a 6.7 percent increase for private institutions. Faculty salaries dropped dramatically in real terms because salary increases were small even though inflation was high (American Association of University Professors, 1992). In general, expenditures per FTES decline during periods of high inflation; faculty salaries invariably lag behind increases in the consumer price index.

A third phase of strong growth in expenditures began during the early 1980s. On average, higher education expenditures per student increased by 2.7 percent annually starting with the 1978–1979 academic year and extending through 1987–1988, adjusted for inflation and enrollment growth, as documented in a study of 2,045 colleges and universities by Getz and

Siegfried (1992, p. 300). Such growth was fueled primarily by tuition increases, which outpaced inflation, and secondarily by state appropriations, which reached an inflation-adjusted high in 1986–1987 of $4,257 for public institutions (Research Associates of Washington, 1992b, p. 8). The largess was used chiefly to restore the purchasing power of salaries, which had eroded during the preceding decade; to reduce the teaching load of regular faculty at universities where research was a major responsibility; to expand the size of administrations; to meet the costs of increasing government regulation and expensive litigation; to increase access for underrepresented groups and promote cultural diversity; to provide more institutionally based student financial aid; and to purchase and maintain computers and other devices of high technology (Massy and Zemsky, 1990a, 1990b; MacPherson, 1991; National Association of College and University Business Officers, 1991).

A fourth phase started in 1990, with a rapid decline in state support (even in nominal dollars) and the stringency imposed throughout higher education by national recession. There is no doubt that most institutions—no matter how large or prestigious they are—now face difficult decisions about resources.

Have Federal and State Appropriations Kept Pace with Resource Needs in Higher Education?

The diversity of higher education is most apparent in the array of funding sources and its many clienteles. The popular conception is that students are higher education's primary clients, but their tuition and fees provide only 24 percent of revenues for all colleges and universities. Endowment interest, private contracts, and donors provide 7.82 percent of the total. Those who purchase institutional services—whether they are individuals buying books or corporations buying research—provide 25 percent of all institutional revenues.

Of course, the largest share of support for higher education comes from taxpayers. American state, local, and federal governments spent almost $60 billion in 1989–1990, more than 42 percent of higher education's current fund income (*Chronicle of Higher Education,* 1992, p. 34). So it is appropriate to ask whether the support that higher education has received from governments has kept pace with the demands that they have placed on it. This is no easy question to answer, since public support is complicated by the myriad relationships of government finance. A definitive analysis would isolate specific government policies (such as promoting vocational education at the state level or encouraging the neediest students at the federal level) and investigate the funding adequacy for each policy over time. However, without a detailed analysis of this kind, we can reach some general conclusions.

Role of States. Under the U.S. Constitution, the states have primary responsibility for education. Collectively, states provide more than 40 percent of the educational and general revenues for all colleges and universities and almost 60 percent of the revenues for public institutions. Most states also have either direct or indirect control over the tuition policies of public colleges and universities, so that declines in appropriations are often offset by increased student charges to maintain the level of institutional revenues. Further, two important shifts in state support have occurred over the years. First, states now provide a larger proportion of the budgets for two-year colleges than for other institutions, where, nationwide during the 1970s, "funding shifted appreciably from local to state governmental sources" (National Center for Education Statistics, 1984, p. 64). Second, some states, notably those in the northeast, have large numbers of private institutions and provide tax support directly to them and large amounts of financial aid to their students.

Table 1.1 provides evidence of the dramatic change in state funding for higher education between the 1980s and 1990s. During the 1980s, state educational appropriations per student (excluding funding for organized research, agricultural extension, and teaching hospitals) increased by 6.2 percent in inflation-adjusted dollars. However, higher education funding under the control of state policy increased by more than this during the same period as the result of a 30 percent increase in tuition revenues per student.

Table 1.1. State Support for Higher Education During Phases Three and Four

Revenue Element	1980–1981	1989–1990	Inflation-Adjusted	Percentage Change
Educational appropriations per student	$2,450	$4,265	$2,602	6.20
Net tuition per student	$673	$1,428	$871	29.45
Educational appropriations and tuition per student	$3,123	$5,694	$3,474	11.23
HEPI (base year = 1982–1983)	85.9	140.8		63.91

Revenue Element	1989–1990	1991–1992	HEPI	Percentage Change
Educational appropriations per student	$4,265	$4,257	$3,915	−8.21
Net tuition per student	$1,428	$1,655	$1,522	6.59
Educational appropriations and tuition per student	$5,694	$5,912	$5,437	−4.51
HEPI (base year = 1982–1983)	140.80	153.10		8.74

Note: HEPI = Higher Education Price Index.

Sources: Research Associates of Washington, 1992a, p. 32; 1992b, pp. 168–170.

Since 1989, however, state appropriations have plummeted. Through 1992, institutions of higher education have received 8.2 percent less per student in educational appropriations adjusted for inflation. The overall decline in state funding was slightly lower only because large tuition increases continued. By any measure, the 1990s began with unprecedented declines in state support.

Federal Role. Assessing the federal contribution to higher education is more difficult. Rather than shouldering continuing responsibility for the basic operations of postsecondary institutions, the federal government intervenes periodically, albeit massively, to promote what officials consider to be the national interest, providing funding in specific areas before turning to support other programs.

Higher education is scheduled to receive roughly $27 billion from federal sources in fiscal 1993, but this money is concentrated in student financial aid and research. Viewed from the perspective of several decades, the federal contribution is truly impressive. Since 1963–1964, two years before the Great Society legislation, federal funds for student financial aid have increased twenty-two fold, even when adjusted for inflation, although not for enrollment increases (Clotfelter, 1992, p. 99). Federal student aid, which today exceeds $25 billion if federally guaranteed loans are included, represents more than three-fourths of student aid available from all sources (Hauptman, 1991, p. 114). But these aggregate amounts hide the enormous shift from grants to loans. Almost all of the net increase in federal student financial aid since 1975 has come in the form of loans, which rose from an annual $1 billion in 1975 to $14 billion in fiscal 1991 (Frances, 1992, p. 27).

Federal funding for university research in fiscal 1993 is roughly $12 billion, or nearly $14 billion if federally funded research and development centers are included (Hauptman, 1991, p. 114). These funds represent about 60 percent of all funds for academic research and development, although the federal government has decreased its proportion of total university research from 75 percent in the 1960s to 65 percent today (Hauptman, 1991, p. 114; National Association of College and University Business Officers, 1991, p. 10). The shift toward defense-related research has been clear. The ratio between defense and nondefense research was about 1:1 from 1965 to 1980, but by 1986–1987, the balance had shifted to 70 percent defense, 30 percent nondefense (Hartle, 1990, p. 35). Although the end of the Cold War halted the growth in defense-related research, the proportion has changed little.

The pattern of federal support has generally been erratic. Higher education's total of federal funds grew fastest under the Nixon and Ford administrations, when the annual rate of increase, adjusted for inflation but not for enrollment, exceeded 9 percent, primarily because of the Vietnam era increase in GI Bill benefits. Although federal aid was made available to middle-income students, federal higher education funds fell slightly in real terms under the Carter administration, since, among other factors, the GI benefits declined substantially. The Reagan administration presided over a 2 percent annual inflation-adjusted decline in federal spending for higher education. Nevertheless, higher education appropriations represented nearly 8 percent of the federal discretionary budget (the funds beyond entitlement), up from 5 percent in 1980 (Hauptman, 1991, pp. 118–120).

How Should Institutions Determine Resource Scarcity?

Resources are *scarce* when they are insufficient to accomplish a certain task. Scarcity refers to the difference between factors that, when combined, will accomplish certain policy goals and the fiscal, human, and capital resources that are available to accomplish those goals. Resources are *adequate* when these factors will accomplish a policy goal at an acceptable level of quality.

It is important to understand that a calculation of adequacy involves more than a cost study or ratio analysis (Brinkman and Allen, 1986; Dickmeyer, 1980; Dickmeyer and Hughes, 1987; Taylor, 1984). The concepts of scarcity and adequacy require an evaluation that identifies policy goals, quality levels, efficiency standards, factors of production, and available resources. This is a powerful tool for analyzing resources in a larger context than traditional cost studies. It is more complicated, but it has greater benefits for planning and evaluation than other approaches. Only a brief outline of what can be termed *resource evaluation* is possible here.

Principles. Principles for resource evaluation studies have emerged from the work of administrators and analysts in higher education who want cost data to make a difference in managing their institutions. First, the purpose of a resource study should be clear and consequential. The results should have the potential to make a real difference in future decisions. Second, each institution should define its own policies and its own level of acceptable quality and effectiveness before evaluating its resources. There is no absolute standard of resource adequacy in higher education. Third, a college or university should focus initially on discrete aspects of its operation (such as lower-division instruction), not on aggregate measures (such as its expenditures per full-time-equivalent student). We can evaluate resource adequacy more effectively when we use several relatively homogeneous activities as building blocks in the process of determining the total resources required for all policy goals.

Steps. The complicated process of resource evaluation is best conducted through a series of steps. The first step is to identify a complete set of policy goals whose accomplishment can be measured and associated with specific costs. For example, the distinctive policy goals of colleges and universities may be to serve the nation's best students in the liberal arts, offer a full array of high-quality professional programs, have the region's leading graduate programs in the sciences, prepare students well for transfer to a four-year institution, serve primarily full-time students in residence near the campus, maintain a policy of "need-blind" admissions, conduct remedial education only for freshmen, increase research grants, ensure that each graduate is computer literate, and maintain a low student-faculty ratio at the lower-division level. The universal policy goals may be to have a student body that reflects the demographic diversity of the community, operate the business service functions efficiently, maintain the physical plant adequately, and use technology to its maximum potential.

The second step is to identify certain measures of acceptable quality, for example, an average student-faculty ratio for each level of instruction (including televised courses); the level of faculty salaries that will allow the institution to compete successfully with others; the library resources needed for each area of the curriculum; the amount of research and scholarship expected of faculty; the extent of instructional equipment and computing support necessary for students to become skillful with the tools of their future occupations.

Step three is to develop a set of comparison institutions for each major area of investigation. Each comparison set should consist of institutions that share at least one important characteristic with the college or university that is conducting the evaluation. For example, one set might consist of institutions with a similar mission; another, of similar size; another, of similar control (public or private); another, of similar student demographics (residential, part-time, older, multiethnic, and so forth); and still another, of competitors for faculty. Brinkman (1987) is especially helpful when specific institutions have to be selected for study. If data from comparison institutions are carefully collected and appropriately adjusted so as to make them congruent with the policies of the institution conducting the study, they are invaluable for understanding what an activity should cost. The new approaches of benchmarking and activity-based accounting are also promising in this regard (Coate and Shafer, 1992).

Step four is to collect longitudinal data in each area. A cost study should compare costs over several years with those at other institutions. The investigator should be careful to select an appropriate initial year, since the length of a time series can have a powerful influence on conclusions (Pickens, 1986).

Step five is to take the effect of inflation correctly into account when evaluating resource adequacy over time. Time series data must take inflation into account. This aim is best accomplished by unbundling the institution's activities. As Table 1.2 shows, inflation has different impacts on the various items purchased in higher education.

Since 1980, costs for supplies and materials increased the least (39.6 percent), while the cost of fringe benefits increased the most (167 percent). Educational expenditures are traditionally organized by program category (instruction, academic support, and so forth) and by object category (salaries, fringe benefits, utilities, library materials, and so forth). Research into inflation's impact best begins with the object categories and applies inflation

Table 1.2. Measures of Price Changes for Various Expenditure Categories in Higher Education, 1980–1992

	1980	1992	Twelve-Year Increase
Professional salaries	79.4	160.8	102.52%
Nonprofessional salaries	80.2	140.4	75.06%
Fringe benefits	72.6	193.9	167.08%
Services	76.5	144.6	89.02%
Supplies and materials	84.6	118.1	39.60%
Equipment	81.6	125.9	54.29%
Library acquisitions	79.5	189.9	138.87%
Utilities	64.1	89.4	39.47%
Higher education price index	77.5	153.1	97.55%

Source: Research Associates of Washington, 1992a, p. 32.

indexes specific to each category of expenditure. The best measures in this regard come from the Higher Education Price Index, published by Research Associates of Washington, which totals the twenty-five components of cost most common to college and university budgets (Halstead, 1983; Research Associates of Washington, 1992a).

The last step is to take technological change and trade-offs into account. The longer a time series is, the less comparable expenditures are because of, in the jargon of economists, the changing contributions of inputs—especially the relative productivity of capital and labor. Technology has influenced cost patterns in highly visible ways, such as when the library's card catalog is automated or touch-tone registration is installed, and in less obvious but still important ways, such as when personal computers gradually appear around campus. These changes should be recognized when resource adequacy is measured in relation to policy goals.

Colleges and universities often change the amount and quality of the commodities and labor that they purchase, which complicates the analysis of expenditures when an inflation measure is applied: "To the extent that [institutions] . . . use different pedagogy, analyses, instruments, equipment, and materials from year to year or that institutions employ different mixes of personnel and capital to accomplish objectives, use of a fixed-weight index fails to price current actual practices" (Research Associates of Washington, 1992a, p. 10). For those who must cope with this challenge, this is a good rule: Never assume that a policy goal can only be accomplished through a fixed set of factors with a constant price relationship; resource adequacy is a dynamic measure, and analysis should recognize this fact.

A Look Ahead

Over the last forty years, distinguished authors have warned that American higher education was facing a major crisis or standing at some critical crossroads. Despite some exaggerated alarms, these authors have been right: Fiscal vicissitudes have changed the institutions of higher education since 1950, especially in where they receive revenues and in how they spend them.

During the 1980s, higher education enjoyed a vigorous growth in resources fueled by tuition increases and state appropriations. Clearly, this expansion of real resources will not continue in the foreseeable future. State appropriations are declining, and it is doubtful that double-digit increases in tuition are a permanent feature of higher education finance. Colleges and universities cannot meet the many responsibilities that they have assumed with their existing finances or through their current organization.

For state governments, the contours of this new era are clear: Higher education is not likely to regain the share of state expenditures that it once received. The five-year projections from Research Associates of Washington (1992a) are illuminating in this regard. Many states have loosened policy and regulatory controls on public institutions and begun to downplay access as their first priority. Some states have openly exhorted their institutions to pursue other resources in ways previously considered unbecoming for public institutions or to "reinvent" themselves to maintain services in ways that can reduce taxpayer support.

For the federal government, the contours of this new era are not as clear, because the administration has changed. Nevertheless, everyone agrees that the total amount of federal support for higher education will not increase in real dollars because of the compelling demands of a decaying infrastructure; the pressing need for health care reform; the priority accorded to K–12 education, vocational training, and worker retraining; and the galloping growth of the federal debt. Within the current levels of support, important changes are almost certain: Defense-related research should decline rapidly, to be replaced by increased funding for health research (with an emphasis on AIDS), programs in high-performance computing, and environmental research. Vocational training and worker retraining, cooperative education, national technology policy, and economic development are likely to take center stage during President Clinton's first term, not such initiatives as the 1988 Academic Facilities Modernization Program. Student aid grants are unlikely to receive more attention than they have in the past, while income-contingent forgivable loans and education in exchange for national service appear to be the new directions in student financial aid.

The President's Council of Advisors on Science and Technology issued a report after the national election on the federal role in university research (Cordes, 1993). In explaining the report, Harold T. Shapiro, president of Princeton University, offered poignant advice for research-intensive universities that is appropriate beyond the boundaries of research: "We urge each university to adopt a strategy for itself, based on a realistic appraisal of future resources, and to commit to meet world-class standards in all programs that they decide to keep or begin" (Cordes, 1993, p. A26). The concepts of resource evaluation and scarcity can help us in adopting this strategy and in meeting our present crisis.

References

American Association of University Professors. "Diversity Within Adversity: The Annual Report on the Economic Status of the Profession, 1991–92." *Academe,* 1992, *78* (2), 7–89.

Bowen, H. R. *The Costs of Higher Education.* San Francisco: Jossey-Bass, 1980.

Brinkman, P. T. (ed.). *Conducting Interinstitutional Comparisons.* New Directions for Institutional Research, no. 53. San Francisco: Jossey-Bass, 1987.

Brinkman, P. T. "College and University Adjustments to a Changing Financial Environment." In S. A. Hoenack and E. L. Collins (eds.), *The Economics of American Universities.* Albany: State University of New York Press, 1990.

Brinkman, P. T., and Allen, R. H. "Concepts of Cost and Cost Analysis for Higher Education." *AIR Professional File,* 1986, *23,* 1–8.

Cartter, A. M. *Ph.D.'s and the Academic Labor Market.* New York: McGraw-Hill, 1976.

Cheit, E. F. *The New Depression in Higher Education: Two Years Later.* New York: McGraw-Hill, 1973.

Chronicle of Higher Education Editors Staff. *Almanac of Higher Education.* Chicago: University of Chicago Press, 1992.

Clotfelter, C. T. "Financial Aid and Public Policy." In C. T. Clotfelter and others (eds.), *Economic Challenges in Higher Education.* Chicago: University of Chicago Press, 1992.

Coate, E., and Shafer, B. S. "Benchmarking in Higher Education." *NACUBO Business Officer,* 1992, *26* (5), 28–35.

Cordes, C. "Bush Science Panel Says Universities Should Brace for More Tough Choices." *Chronicle of Higher Education,* Jan. 6, 1993, p. A26.

Dickmeyer, N. *Ratio Analysis in Higher Education.* New York: Peat Marwick Mitchell, 1980.

Dickmeyer, N., and Hughes, K. S. *Financial Self-Assessment: A Workbook for Colleges and Universities.* Washington, D.C.: National Association of College and University Business Officers, 1987.

Frances, C. *A Chartbook of Trends Affecting Higher Education Finance, 1960–1990.* Westport, Conn.: Common Fund Press, 1992.

Froomkin, J. "The Impact of Changing Financial Resources." In S. A. Hoenack and E. L. Collins (eds.), *The Economics of American Universities.* Albany: State University of New York Press, 1990.

Getz, M., and Siegfried, J. J. "Cost Inflation." In C. T. Clotfelter and others (eds.), *Economic Challenges in Higher Education.* Chicago: University of Chicago Press, 1992.

Halstead, K. D. *Inflation Measures for Schools and Colleges.* Washington, D.C.: Government Printing Office, 1983.

Halstead, K. D. *Higher Education Revenues and Expenditures: A Study of Institutional Costs.* Vol. 1. Washington, D.C.: Research Associates of Washington, 1991.

Hartle, T. "Federal Support for Higher Education in the 90s: Boom, Bust, or Something in Between?" *Change,* 1990, *22* (1), 32–41.

Hauptman, A. M. "Trends in the Federal and State Financial Commitment to Higher Education." In D. H. Finifter and others (eds.), *The Uneasy Public Policy Triangle in Higher Education.* New York: Macmillan, 1991.

MacPherson, R. A. "Covering All the Bases: A Model Hazardous Waste Program for Small Universities." *NACUBO Business Officer,* 1991, *25* (5), 48–51.

Massy, W., and Zemsky, R. "Cost Containment: Committing to a New Economic Reality." *Change Magazine,* 1990a, *22* (6), 16–27.

Massy, W., and Zemsky, R. "The Lattice and the Ratchet." *Policy Perspectives,* 1990b, *2* (4), 1–8.

National Association of College and University Business Officers. *Government Policy and Regulation: An Executive Briefing Paper.* Washington, D.C.: National Association of College and University Business Officers, 1991.

National Center for Education Statistics. *The Condition of Education: A Statistical Report, 1984 Edition.* Washington, D.C.: Government Printing Office, 1984.

Pickens, W. H. "Funding over Time: Measuring Institutional Finance." In P. M. Callan (ed.), *Environmental Scanning for Strategic Leadership.* New Directions for Institutional Research, no. 52. San Francisco: Jossey-Bass, 1986.

Research Associates of Washington. *Inflation Measures for Schools and Colleges: 1992 Update.* Washington, D.C.: Research Associates of Washington, 1992a.

Research Associates of Washington. *State Profiles: Financing Public Higher Education, 1978 to 1992.* Washington, D.C.: Research Associates of Washington, 1992b.

Taylor, B. "Monitoring the Financial Condition of Colleges and Universities." *AAHE Bulletin,* Dec. 1984, pp. 7–10.

U.S. Department of Education. *1992 Back to School Forecast: Press Release.* Washington, D.C.: Government Printing Office, 1992.

WILLIAM H. PICKENS *is associate vice president for administration at California State University, Sacramento, and formerly was director of fiscal analysis for the California Postsecondary Education Commission and executive director of the commission.*

The first response to a sudden reduction in resources is defensive, but constructive adjustments for the intermediate period and new directions for the long term are worth exploring.

Significant Options for Primarily Instructional Institutions

William B. Simpson

Working with scarce resources is a commonplace problem. We are particularly concerned when resources become significantly scarce, since this impairs the education of our students with whose well-being we identify and denies benefits to society, which we seek to advance.

Defensive Reaction

How are we to react to sudden and substantial budget cuts that affect the extent and quality of ongoing operations in higher education (Simpson, 1992b)? The strategy that perhaps comes first to mind is to make highly visible cuts in services that will cause the most outcry—closing campuses and limiting enrollment—so that allies come forward to oppose the reduction. But such reductions could hurt students more than moves in other directions, and those who react in this manner could appear to be poorly advised and lose their credibility. Moreover, the resources needed to make up for such cuts may simply not be available.

There may be expenditures that could be trimmed with minimal damage to the educational enterprise—the proverbial limousines used by administrators, country club fees, catered lunches, exorbitant retirement packages, and so forth. If the institution has such expenditures and if it has encountered periods of scarcity more than once, it is likely that corrective adjustments have already been made. If adjustments have not been made, such expenditures can hinder efforts to obtain public support.

Another reaction is to shift expenses onto users by instituting new fees or raising existing fees for services. Such measures can work hardship on students, who are less able to pay such fees than the average taxpayer. Also, they are likely to limit the extent to which students undertake higher education, an effect that harms society at large. One alternative is to raise tuition selectively by field. Such a move need not deter pursuit of the optimum extent of education if it takes into account field-specific differences both in the cost of instruction and in the extent to which the benefit to society is capturable as personal benefit (Simpson, 1991). Such remedies as raising fees for units beyond the minimum required for a degree or for units toward a second terminal degree are to be avoided because they limit students' ability to adapt to changes in the job market.

Some adjustments could be lived with if we knew that the reduction in support would be of short duration. For example, we could postpone paying bills, not transfer payments into self-insurance funds, draw down inventories of supplies, postpone maintenance and repairs, leave library journals unbound and interrupt subscriptions, cut library hours, delay cost-of-living salary adjustments, postpone improvements in fringe benefits, leave personnel vacancies temporarily unfilled or shift to part-time or temporary personnel, postpone expenditures for instructional technology, postpone investment in new buildings or new campuses, and so forth. Postponing capital outlay may not be helpful, since measures authorizing the issuance of bonds may have been passed even though operating budgets have been constrained.

All of these measures have a cost: interest charges, deterioration that cannot be repaired, lost opportunities to provide education or increase long-term efficiency, lowered effectiveness and morale, and so forth. They do not provide a permanent solution. To the extent that it is possible to catch up, it could cost more to catch up than it does to meet costs currently.

Even when we know that resource scarcity is not temporary, the absence of contingency plans may require us to adopt one or more of the measures just reviewed in order to buy time in which to develop and act upon other measures.

A strategy that contrasts with cutting where there will be the most outcry is to make the pain politically tolerable by spreading it as evenly as possible. Uniform across-the-board budget cuts are one such means. Across-the-board cuts can be adopted either to buy time, as just suggested, or on the assumption that every operation has some slack. For example, there are more than a dozen ways to economize in scheduling multiple sections for a course (Simpson, 1991). However, across-the-board cuts, for which Bowen (1983) gives additional arguments, are changes that are waiting to be reversed.

Across-the-board adjustments for the programs that we retain are not as simple as they may seem to be. As I have explained elsewhere (Simpson, 1981), career step increments within a rank, promotions, and selective salary increases for special merit should be awarded before any across-the-board reductions in cost-of-living adjustments or salary rates are made to ensure that salary relationships among the parties concerned are appropriate. Moreover, those in lower ranks should be subject to a lesser percentage reduction.

Cuts in the number of positions should first be made among support staff and among part-time and probationary faculty. Staff should not be cut by an equal percentage across all programs, since cuts have a greater impact on small programs. Moreover, exceptions may have to be made to preserve recent advances in gender and minority representativeness. Termination of younger faculty can be reduced by increasing incentives for senior faculty and administrators to retire early (Magner, 1992). To prevent excessively heavy turnover within an academic or administrative area, the program should not be entirely optional.

Cutbacks in personnel imply cuts in courses and class sections, reduced summer offerings, and—unless enrollment is limited—increased class size. Students will need to attend longer in order to obtain the courses required for graduation.

Various of these adjustments take time, not only for the decision process itself but also so that proper notice can be given, the retraining involved in lateral transfers can be completed, and programs can be adjusted accordingly. The publication *Policy Documents and Reports* (American Association of University Professors, 1990) outlines the applicable standards. Elsewhere (Simpson, 1974), I have discussed options in personnel adjustments in question-and-answer format. While the options discussed therein concern reductions in force arising from declines in enrollment within particular fields, they are applicable to adjustments forced by declining overall support.

Constructive Structuring and Flexibility

After people have been made aware that the institution faces scarce resources, they must take a new look at the ways in which resources are being used. Such a situation creates opportunities for channeling effort into constructive initiatives improving the ways in which the objectives sought are obtained. Indeed, the situation makes it possible to make changes—improvements—that could not readily be obtained in the absence of pressure. The parties affected should be represented in deliberations on a solution, as discussed in Gappa (this volume).

Decisions as to what goals to serve are not purely economic, nor are decisions as to the extent to which each goal should be pursued. But to the extent that such decisions can be cast in economic form, individual goals should be pursued to such an extent as will maximize the total net benefit in combination. An individual goal is pursued to the optimal extent when a marginal change in the level of pursuit brings equal and opposite effects upon benefit and cost. Interdependence among the activities has to be considered. Cost includes the foregone benefits of activities that have to be curtailed.

Resources tend to be used most effectively through choice of an appropriate combination of a structure as to the goals to be served and flexibility, possibly within a framework of regulations, as to the means employed to serve them. Structure enables us to realize the economies forthcoming from specialization and focus. Flexibility within a structure enables us to use the most cost-effective combination of inputs.

Structure. The designation of a campus or a separate system of campuses for the conduct of research combined with graduate instruction is an example of structure as I use the term here. Faculty engage in research as part of their work load alongside instruction, and they undertake research under contract to external sources of support. Froomkin (this volume) discusses the difficult choices facing research universities in undertaking cost containment.

Resources are often structured by campus according to instructional areas covered, such as the health professions, law, education, or business or, more broadly, vocational, technical, liberal arts, or professional subjects. Cost can be reduced by eliminating duplication among institutions within an urban area. Institutional cost can also be reduced by having institutions in different regions of a state develop specialized offerings and by relying on students to travel or relocate in order to obtain the instructional program desired. Opposition to specialization within public institutions has been raised in Massachusetts (Jaschik, 1992).

Selective depth of offering modifies the specialization approach. Under this strategy, each institution offers basic courses in a wide array of fields and a range of majors and minors, but a full complement of supporting courses, together with distinguished faculty in the particular field, is available at only a limited number of institutions selected in part for geographical reasons. This strategy reduces, but does not entirely eliminate, duplicate course offerings. A system that adopts this strategy should make sure that each campus provides the courses in nonemphasized fields required by its emphasized fields.

The strategy just outlined is a useful compromise when budgetary stringency forces the institution to choose between maintaining the full range of offerings or maintaining the quality of the programs offered by narrowing the range. Adoption of this approach poses both immediate and transitional problems for students and faculty in the programs that are curtailed. The recent controversy at San Diego State University (Abdelnour, 1992) and the case of the State University of New York (American Association of University Professors, 1977; Volkwein, 1984) illustrate these problems.

A cluster of colleges in a given geographical area can reduce cost by using the selective depth approach and by other interinstitutional arrangements (Gaff and Associates, 1970; Simpson, 1991). When members of a consortium are relatively distant, a student might study at different campuses in different terms (Patterson, 1974). For example, each college in the Claremont College cluster has a specialized focus. Cross-registration minimizes the need for duplicate course offerings. Each college builds a distinguished faculty in its particular fields. The close proximity of the colleges, together with joint operation of selected administrative functions and common library and other facilities, achieves economy combined with ready access to excellent facilities.

Even among institutions that are not part of a formal grouping, arrangements could be made in advance for students to enroll on an individual ad hoc basis at another public or private institution, particularly for upper-division and graduate courses, when there is insufficient enrollment to justify the offering of certain courses in a given term at a particular campus. If the arrangement is not sufficiently reciprocal, there could be financial remuneration between the institutions.

Although interlibrary electronic access enables institutions to economize on the number of publications purchased, it forces publishers either to raise prices or to turn away manuscripts having a limited readership. Both developments have the effect of reducing access for library users and cost savings for libraries.

Another type of structuring is reflected in the community college movement, which relies on two-year institutions that are readily accessible geographically. Redirecting first-year applicants at four-year institutions to the significantly less costly community colleges can reduce the cost of education for a state (Mercer, 1992). However, such redirection may force students to choose between an academic and a vocational career sooner than they would have to if they had enrolled in a four-year institution. And diverting individuals from the fullest development of their capabilities may have costs for society.

Resources can also be structured around time of use. For example, institutions can choose between a two-semester nine-month calendar (with a separately financed summer session) and a trimester or four-quarter academic calendar that makes regular academic courses available throughout the year. In addition to bringing benefits to students, year-round operation can economize on capital outlay by spreading use of physical facilities over the year. Saving on capital outlay may not have high priority, but it does reduce the cost of additional debt service. What may reduce enthusiasm for conversion to year-round operation when budgets are tight is the forward acceleration of operating costs, since individuals complete more units of education each year. There are also additional costs during the conventional nine months to accommodate demands made on staff time by the extended program, and these additional costs must be met in subsequent budget periods if the move to year-round operation is not to impair the quality of the education that can be offered. It is particularly important to protect against staff fatigue and to give faculty members opportunities to keep current in their field. Planning models for year-round operation are available (Simpson, 1973).

Education can also be structured as on or off campus. (Off-campus education includes distance education.) Distance education has lower operating costs per instructional unit. Moreover, it has lower interest cost, since capital outlay is less. However, distance education should not be emphasized solely with the thought of reducing total expenditure, since total cost rises as a result of the greater number served (Simpson, 1991). Distance education can be justified financially if its fees make it self-supporting or even if the deficit at which it operates is less than the marginal cost of teaching those who would otherwise have attended on campus.

Flexibility. When the total financial resources for instruction are relatively fixed for a given period, as they are when a budget has been agreed upon, subordinate decision levels must have flexibility in deciding how to use resources within the structure that has been established.

Academic units operate subject to budgets that were put together earlier, yet they face current and prospective changes in the extent and nature of the services demanded. Changes may be needed in the configuration of lectures, labs, and discussion sections and in the combination of live presentations with instructional technology (Simpson, 1991). These changes affect class size and the frequency of course offerings. Norris and MacDonald (this volume) and I (Simpson, this volume, Chapter Seven) examine the promise offered by new technology for cost reduction and the limitations of that promise.

Elsewhere (Simpson, 1975), I have discussed how the need for change in faculty staffing can be accommodated in the current period and also be incorporated into budgets being developed for subsequent periods. The constrained ratio approach advocated there is conducive to innovation in instructional practices, and it maintains responsible overall control of resources. It encourages the effective use of resources by structuring the allocative procedure so as to increase the likelihood that those considering options at the instructional level will be aware of the costs in foregone opportunities.

Personnel can be encouraged to seek economies if the operating unit can retain and carry forward in its budget a significant portion of the savings thereby obtained (Carnegie Commission on Higher Education, 1972), especially if the operating unit has some discretion in the use of its share of the savings.

Flexibility within a salary structure makes it possible for the institution to recognize individual merit. However, the moral problems raised by attempts to rank individuals by professional worth are formidable. These problems can be used as reasons for relying on automatic and uniform salary increases. The career increment portion of a salary adjustment should reflect the increase in an individual's value to the institution as a result of the individual's maturation and current position on the learning curve. The individual is responsible for learning not only his or her academic field but also the teaching and other skills that a professional in a university needs. Where flexibility is required is in the recognition of special merit, by which I mean an exceptional increase in capacity for future performance. Such merit is a function not primarily of time and experience but of the extent, direction, and quality of individual effort. It should be regarded as exceptional in relation both to professional standards and to colleagues. Determinations of special merit should present fewer problems than a complete ranking of all faculty. The salary increment can have a significant effect on morale and perhaps on performance. Exceptional performance of a one-time task without relevance to future performance should be rewarded by a one-time bonus, which is much more economical than a permanent upward movement of all future salary payments. A table in Simpson (1981) outlines options in the design of salary structure that can hold down the costs of salary advancement.

Flexibility has dangers when administrative responsibility and status are assigned. Administration has borne the brunt of criticism for escalating operating costs. While a careful study by Hansen and Guidugli (1990) shows that the number of full-time administrative positions increased only slightly between 1975 and 1983 relative to full-time faculty positions, this means that such administrative positions have increased as a variable cost, rather than being more in the nature of a fixed cost. The same period has seen rapid, more than proportional growth in professional nonfaculty positions. These two developments follow in part from the expanded breadth of administrative concerns in recent decades and the attendant increase in reporting functions. The multiplication of administrative levels that we have seen is unwarranted (Bergmann, 1991; Galambos, 1988; Halfond, 1991; Simpson, 1991). Even when a given level retains a reasonable span of policy control, we often see a proliferation of positions for administrators with a narrow range of duties, many of whom repeat and extend that proliferation. Consolidation of administrative positions should produce significant economies.

New technology produces other opportunities for cost savings in the area of administration. The initial outlays for equipment and the operating cost for training must be taken into account. Norris and MacDonald (this volume) discuss these issues, as do Zemsky and Massy (1990).

Longer-Term New Directions

Managing scarce resources when resources are being reduced is often viewed as damage control: The adverse effects are to be held to a minimum. This goal is better accomplished by selective adjustments than it is by proportional across-the-board reductions. At the same time, resources need to be released so that they can be directed into substitute activities, activities that serve alternative or additional goals or that serve existing goals more efficiently.

If it were only a matter of adopting more efficient techniques, we might wonder why the switch could not simply be made, directly reducing cost, improving outcomes, or achieving some combination of these two objectives. But such changes are more complicated than that. Several interrelated aspects of change need skillful programming: Key personnel with the appropriate skills have to be recruited. Equipment and staff training have to be provided. Changes have to be phased in for existing students and faculty and coordinated with other stages of the educational process. Such efforts may need to extend over a period of time before some combination of improved outcomes and reduced cost is evident. Institutional research conducted with the aid of a carefully designed pilot project may provide insights helpful in formulating policies and conducting operations.

Motivating Individuals to Value Education. Higher education's most distinctive opportunity for service lies in countering students' cynicism about their place in society by interpreting the possible roles of intelligence and concern in a world that other influences seem to shape. At a time when efforts both to explore outer space and to improve our own environment have been cut back for budgetary reasons, the university's humanities and other liberal arts offerings give students the opportunity to develop their "inner space" and their sense of context. Surely that is the best investment an individual can make, whatever the future may offer (Simpson, 1974).

Enlisting advanced students, alumni, and current and emeritus faculty in higher education in early mentoring activity in the public schools would be a service of great value. A high school with several thousand students may have only a single staff position that can provide assistance in college planning.

That education makes a difference and that students can make a difference in their lives by investing in their own human capital are emphasized in the program of the Joint Council on Economic Education (1990). The council will work with teachers interested in integrating that message into the curriculum.

Such efforts need to stress that the student may well be the most important influence on whether he or she achieves his or her goals. Persistence is an essential ingredient of success.

Pencavel (1991) used data on consumer income from the U.S. Department of Commerce to show that for each level of schooling earnings increase with age and eventually become constant or decline, that the rate of increase of earnings with age is greater for those who have more schooling, and that the earnings peak comes later in life for those with more education. These findings hold true for men and women alike. Leslie and Brinkman (1988) address the same issue.

Students should not aim for an average level of performance. If they want to be more than average, they must do more than average. Students need to be encouraged to resist the peer group pressures that make them reluctant to stand out by excelling over others and to do more than asked. They need to view themselves as engines of discovery that are self-propelled.

These considerations apply both to advantaged and disadvantaged students within our society. Students from advantaged backgrounds may disregard the importance of their own attitude upon efforts to be educated and still lead a life that is comfortable if not particularly productive. Students from disadvantaged backgrounds disregard the importance of their own attitude at the peril of remaining stuck in their original straits.

It also makes sense for high schools and colleges to remain in contact with individuals who interrupt their education so that they can encourage them to undertake subsequent education—of an informal nature if necessary.

Broadening Educational Options for Minority Youth. In a report for the state of California following the Watts riots in Los Angeles in the 1960s (Simpson, 1967), I made recommendations aimed at reducing the barriers to access to higher education and choice of institution that minority youth encountered. I was concerned not only with geographical and financial barriers but also with academic and motivational barriers. Government efforts along these lines lessened as the situation returned to normal, although the resulting normalcy condemned many to unsatisfying life experiences. Riots returned to Los Angeles in 1992, after which, in an invited proposal forwarded to the Rebuild Los Angeles Task Force (Simpson, 1992a), I identified goals relative to broadening the educational options for minority youth that a consortium of colleges and universities in the area could advance.

First, learning support programs are particularly useful for students who are educationally disadvantaged. Able students should be organized as peer tutors, and such service should be recognized as a type of school service or as paid employment.

Second, the early mentoring activity by those in higher education cited in the preceding section is particularly important for students for whom the expectation that they continue their education is not an already accepted part of their thinking. We need to establish a continuing student-educator relationship conveying the message that somebody cares that the student makes the most of his or her life. Our first efforts should target students at the equivalent of the eighth and ninth grades in public or private schools that qualify by reason of low average family income among attendees, low college-going rate, academic underperformance, and/or low persistence. Each mentor would undertake to meet regularly with the individuals selected for the program, and there should be considerable interchange between students and mentor. This relationship should be maintained through meetings, correspondence, and telephone calls as students move forward through the various educational levels. Mentors should be available on short notice if necessary. This proposal extends an outreach activity initiated by Reed College of Portland on behalf of Hispanic, African American and Asian American youth in middle schools and high schools in the Los Angeles area.

Third, high school students should be helped to develop a forward view of further education through opportunities to become familiar with higher education programs, staff, campuses, and facilities. Presentations should stress how course objectives have relevance to their lives. Institutions can plan programs for students jointly and hold them at a single campus. Programs can combine academic departments and presenters from different institutions.

Assuring That Students Are Prepared to Benefit. Accepting certification by preparatory schools, public or private, that their graduates have been adequately prepared to benefit from college leads in many instances to predictable waste, which can scarcely be condoned when budgets are tight. Inadequate preparation may reflect inadequate academic standards, accumulation of credits from disconnected experiences at various schools, or promotion of pupils who are getting old relative to classmates. In consultation with feeder schools, colleges and universities should require applicants, even those with high grade point averages, to pass tests demonstrating their current competence in basic skills. A student should not be able to offset a low score in one basic skill by a high score in another. Faculty should relate actively to their counterparts in the preparatory schools in preparing for this change. This informational activity should not be limited to staff of the school relations office.

Difficulties should be headed off at an early stage. An outreach program of Reed College shows what can be done. That program, now in its eighth year, serves high school students in several Oregon counties. The program stresses the need for early and adequate preparation in mathematics for a broad array of academic and professional fields. Each year, students, accompanied by instructors, meet on the Reed campus for workshops conducted by faculty members. Participants are assisted by college student tutors. Computers are accessible, and texts and meals are provided.

Until suitable measures are taken broadly across the curriculum and at an early enough stage, higher education will encounter high school graduates who need extensive remediation. How this remediation is organized and where it is located are not as important as having both preparatory schools and colleges participate in its design and as having students in the interim be in preadmission status insofar as college is concerned. Introducing underprepared students into special sections of courses on a college campus is not recommended, since pressure from the budget and scheduling problems can lead underprepared students to be merged into other class sections. Such merging decreases the challenge that the other students experience. I am not ruling out remediation efforts after admission for the types of challenge that students do not encounter at the high school level. I have discussed what higher education should expect of students and what it should expect of itself in connection with efforts to improve cost-effectiveness on the quality side (Simpson, 1991).

Goal-Oriented Learning. It is a broad but surely a reasonably accurate generalization as one progressively considers preschool, grade school, and high school teaching, undergraduate instruction, and graduate work that what attracts individuals onto the staff shifts from being student oriented to being subject matter oriented and then to being research oriented. Whereas the early stages of education attract individuals who are concerned primarily with the development of individual students, the later stages assemble a faculty interested primarily in involvement with their academic field.

While I was a guest at the University of London in 1953, I wrote—too optimistically, it may now be judged—as follows: "It may be correct to say that the slow trend is toward accepting the teacher as a catalyst rather than purveyor, toward stressing development of the evaluative rather than the absorptive capacities of the student, and toward society asking not simply for adjustment but for responsible participation" (Simpson, 1993b, pp. 1–2).

At a time when massive retrenchment is being called for, it is important to keep in mind the vital core that should be protected. I contend that the core should be viewed in terms more of accomplishing specified goals than of maintaining comprehensive coverage of an academic field. The emphasis needs to be less on what is transmitted and more on what is to be accomplished. The shift should be from teaching subject matter to teaching students or, put alternatively, from subject matter–centered teaching to goal-oriented learning. We need to attend less to imparting information and more to teaching how to process information and reach conclusions (Simpson, 1993a, pp. 19–20).

We also need to encourage students to think inductively and creatively. Students are often altogether too passive in waiting for conclusions to be delivered to them and all too unimaginative in conceiving of alternative frameworks that could lead to additional options.

The ability of students to be articulate in the written and spoken word and to think on their feet and argue their views needs to be developed.

Some courses, if suitably taught, could be regarded as substitutable as a vehicle for achieving underlying objectives, such as sensitizing students to the human condition and expanding the boundaries of individual students' concerns. Constructive interaction among individuals should be advanced not only as a responsibility toward fellow members of society but also as a way of achieving the satisfaction that an individual derives from helping others to achieve their goals. Courses in different academic disciplines that facilitated specified learning goals could achieve some economy in course offerings during a given term.

Goal-oriented learning has a number of other aspects: increased emphasis on the human factor in education, release of faculty time for interaction with students by substituting interactive instructional technology for "talking head" lectures, development of small-scale interdisciplinary study and learning communities, and increased emphasis in library services on the encouragement of creativity.

Winter, McClelland, and Stewart (1981) found that a liberal arts college experience furthered certain effects on students more than a state teachers college or urban community college experience. Goal-oriented learning differs from the liberal arts college or professional school approach in that the design of individual courses, and not simply the curriculum as a whole, is looked to for creating the sought-after effects.

Ulbrich (1992), an economist, described as client-centered academics an approach wherein the study of a subject is directed toward providing assistance through policy recommendations and practical applications in areas of interest to a constituency. Such an approach is particularly useful if it is a potential source of funding. When we regard students as our main constituency and our attention is student centered, then goal-oriented learning also falls within the scope of client-centered academics.

One may adhere to subject-oriented teaching as the preferred activity of higher education and still find that goal-oriented learning is a useful guide when severe cutbacks in curriculum offerings cannot be avoided. Goal-oriented learning remains a largely unexplored approach. While it holds promise for a more effective use of resources than present teaching can make, its introduction would require adjustment of the composition of faculty over an extended period.

References

Abdelnour, S. "California Colleges Brace for Big Cuts in State Financing." *Chronicle of Higher Education*, June 17, 1992, pp. 21, 26.

American Association of University Professors. "Academic Freedom and Tenure: The State University of New York." *AAUP Bulletin*, 1977, *63* (3), 237–260.

American Association of University Professors. *Policy Documents and Reports*. Washington, D.C.: American Association of University Professors, 1990.

Bergmann, B. R. "Bloated Administration, Blighted Campuses." *Academe*, 1991, *77* (6), 12–16.

Bowen, H. R. "The Art of Retrenchment." *Academe*, 1983, *69* (1), 21–24.

Carnegie Commission on Higher Education. *The More Effective Use of Resources: An Imperative for Higher Education*. New York: McGraw-Hill, 1972.

Gaff, J. G., and Associates. *The Cluster College*. San Francisco: Jossey-Bass, 1970.

Galambos, E. C. *Higher Education Administrative Costs: Continuing the Study*. Washington, D.C.: Government Printing Office, 1988.

Halfond, J. A. "How to Control Administrative Cost." *Academe*, 1991, *77* (6), 17–19.

Hansen, W. L., and Guidugli, T. F. "Comparing Salary and Employment Gains for Higher Education Administrators and Faculty Members." *Journal of Higher Education*, 1990, *61* (2), 142–159.

Jaschik, S. "Regional Public Colleges Resist Their States' Demands That They Specialize." *Chronicle of Higher Education*, Apr. 22, 1992, pp. 30–31.

Joint Council on Economic Education. *Choices and Changes: Economic Understanding for the "At-Risk" Child*. New York: Joint Council on Economic Education, 1990.

Leslie, L. L., and Brinkman, P. T. *The Economic Value of Higher Education*. New York: Macmillan, 1988.

Magner, D. K. "Colleges Debate Benefits of Early Retirement Plans as a Way to Shrink Budgets and Avoid Layoffs." *Chronicle of Higher Education*, July 29, 1992, pp. 11–12.

Mercer, J. "States Turn to Community Colleges as Route to Bachelor's Degree as Four-Year Campuses Face Tight Budgets and Overcrowding." *Chronicle of Higher Education*, May 6, 1992, p. 28.

Patterson, F. *Colleges in Consort: Institutional Cooperation Through Consortia.* San Francisco: Jossey-Bass, 1974.

Pencavel, J. "Higher Education, Productivity, and Earnings: A Review." *Journal of Economic Education,* 1991, 22 (3), 331–359.

Simpson, W. B. In K. A. Martyn (ed.), *Increasing Opportunities for Disadvantaged Students.* Sacramento: California Joint Legislative Committee on Higher Education, 1967.

Simpson, W. B. *Planning Models for Academic Calendar Change.* Los Angeles: Department of Economics and Statistics, California State University, 1973.

Simpson, W. B. *Options in Steady-State Staffing.* Los Angeles: Office of Vice President for Academic Affairs, California State University, 1974.

Simpson, W. B. "Constrained Ratio Approach to Allocating Instructional Resources." *Socioeconomic Planning Sciences,* 1975, 9 (6), 285–292.

Simpson, W. B. "Faculty Salary Structure for a College or University." *Journal of Higher Education,* 1981, 52 (3), 219–236.

Simpson, W. B. *Cost Containment for Higher Education: Strategies for Public Policy and Institutional Administration.* New York: Praeger, 1991.

Simpson, W. B. "Broadening Educational Options for Minority Youth." Proposal submitted to the Rebuild Los Angeles Task Force, 1992a.

Simpson, W. B. "Retrenchment in California." *AAUP Footnotes,* Fall 1992b, p. 1.

Simpson, W. B. "Higher Education's Role in a New Beginning." *Academe,* 1993a, 79 (1), 17–21.

Simpson, W. B. "A Creed, 1953." In W. B. Simpson, *Toward Intelligent Choice,* unpublished manuscript, California State University, Los Angeles, 1993b.

Ulbrich, H. H. "Can We Make a Place for Client-Centered Academics?" *Academe,* 1992, 78 (3), 15–16.

Volkwein, J. F. "Responding to Financial Retrenchment: Lessons from the Albany Experience." *Journal of Higher Education,* 1984, 54 (3), 389–401.

Winter, D. G., McClelland, D. C., and Stewart, A. J. *A New Case for the Liberal Arts.* San Francisco: Jossey-Bass, 1981.

Zemsky, R., and Massy, W. F. "Cost Containment: Committing to a New Economic Reality." *Change,* 1990, 22 (6), 16–22.

WILLIAM B. SIMPSON is emeritus professor of economics at California State University, Los Angeles, and formerly was managing editor and coeditor of Econometrica *and executive director of the Cowles Commission for Research in Economics at the University of Chicago.*

Transforming the role of faculty member from one of lecturer to learning facilitator and increasing the student's own responsibility for learning— changes facilitated by increased use of technology—are at the heart of productivity improvement in instruction. Use of technology in administration should emphasize decentralized systems and more sophisticated campus data networks.

Evaluating the Increased Use of Technology in Instruction and Administration

William C. Norris, Geraldine MacDonald

A. Increased Use of Technology in Instruction

The costs of education continue to escalate, but there is no evidence that quality is being increased, let alone maintained. Relatively little attention is given to productivity. Yet colleges are closing their doors because they have failed to address that issue. Campuses are eliminating academic departments not because the departments are not good but because leadership has failed to maintain or enhance productivity. Attention to both productivity and quality can ensure that people have affordable access to the education they need.

Technology is a vital tool for productivity and quality. The array of technology for educational purposes includes computers, interactive video and audio equipment, telecommunications equipment, technology-based courseware for the delivery of instruction, courseware authoring systems, and computer software for managing instruction. These technologies can be applied individually or in combination, as when computer-based interactive video instruction is delivered via a distance learning network or videodisks are controlled by computer.

When faculty use technology at the course level in instructing students or in managing instruction, both students and faculty gain independence and efficiency. Moreover, faculty, students, and institution all benefit from the improved decision making that results when students have more information about themselves and their courses of study and when faculty have more information about students and their performance. Technology can provide such information. A number of universities have established an electronic campus (Rickman and Hubbard, 1992), which consists of a network connecting student rooms, faculty, and administrative offices. Easy access to computing applications, educational video, communications among students, and other services is provided via computer terminals or personal computers.

Students benefit from technology not only in day-to-day efficiencies but also in preparing for a world that will expect them to be conversant with technology. Access to word processing, spreadsheets, and data bases helps students in their daily work, and they should be able to use computer modeling to solve research problems or take an entire course through computer-based materials. In the world of work, computers provide access to a broad range of information and enable users to apply this information in problem solving in myriad ways. To be successful in an information-based economy, students must be prepared to use the technology in normal, day-to-day problem solving while they are still in school.

Cost has historically been a major obstacle to the implementation of technology programs. However, its significance is decreasing. Basic personal computers are now available for less than $1000 each, with promise of further price decreases as the cost of microcircuit chips drops (price reductions have averaged more than 25 percent per year over the past decade). Software and courseware capabilities continue to grow. Students often have access to lease-buy programs spread out over four years of study that allow them to purchase their own personal computers, and institutions can get substantial discounts on computers and software when they buy in quantity. These tools will be necessary after graduation for the most productive professional careers.

As a consequence of the decreasing cost and increasing capabilities of technology, its use is expanding. Increasingly intensive student use of technology can reduce the average cost per student for an institution. However, this expansion is taking place mainly in the form of additions to the traditional education system. Accordingly, the total cost of instruction will reflect not only the lower average cost per student for traditional uses but also the additional cost per student from add-on applications and—not to be overlooked—the additional students who can be served.

Using technology as an add-on has brought benefits, but they fall far short of the potential. Instead, technology must become an integral part of a transformed system in which the faculty member is not a lecturer but a manager and facilitator and in which students assume much of the responsibility for learning. While this major transition should be implemented gradually, it must be given priority if it is to achieve timely progress.

Transforming Tools and Processes

One cornerstone of the transforming process is a personalized learning plan. Other major tools and processes required for the transformation of education are the maximum appropriate use of technology-based learning resources, commonality of technology-based learning resources, technology-based distance learning, and continuous quality improvement.

Personalized Learning Plan. Personalized instruction has long been seen as a key element in effective learning (Fletcher, 1992). However, widespread adoption of personalized learning plans (PLPs) had to await the advent of relatively low-cost high-power technology. Cost-effective utilization of PLPs based on the characteristics and needs of individual students requires comprehensive computer management software, such as the commercially available Personalized Education Management System (PEMS). Faculty members use the software to assemble course curricula, monitor student progress, and provide tutoring when needed (N.E. Metro Technical College, 1992) or to lead groups discussing creative ideas. At the same time, students can access their individual course status as well as their current list of assignments and responsibilities. Personalized instruction allows students to spend more time on new or difficult areas, less time on areas that they have already mastered, and in other ways assume more responsibility for their learning.

Expanding Faculty Options. The PEMS management software enables each faculty member to set up individual course curricula with the computer. Course goals and objectives can be stored and indexed at any level of specificity. Faculty can create instructional materials of different levels of difficulty and stipulate either a selection or a set of required materials for each objective. Multiple assessments and evaluations giving the faculty member a clear organizational structure and the student a total picture of requirements for course completion can also be specified.

Once a course curriculum is in the computer, faculty can make additions and revisions quickly and easily. All course goals, objectives, materials, and assessments are in a single document, the curriculum report. Custom reporting options can help any faculty member fill specific information needs related to courses or students.

Student performance information for both assignments and assessments is entered directly into the computer. PEMS compares the performance information with faculty achievement criteria and updates all associated objectives and goals for a student. Students or faculty can monitor student performance in a variety of ways for any selection of courses, goals, objectives, assignments, or assessments.

Some faculty fear that the technology environment will constrain them. However, as they become at ease with computers, they often find that the technology helps them to explore new methods and even new ideas that are not possible in classrooms where chalkboards and paper predominate.

Expanding Student Options. Each student has an on-line personal learning plan that shows every course, goal, and objective; all assignments; and all assessments for which the student is responsible. The program updates this personal learning plan any time new assignment, assessment, or performance information is entered into the system. Thus, the student can obtain an accurate status report of his or her performance in any course at any time and, if needed, take actions to improve it.

The student also receives a listing of all assignments and assessments to be completed. The software is so flexible that the instructor can give the student the option of choosing among course segments, assignments, or even assessment options. One important feature of the PEMS software is that the faculty member can specify one of three levels of student independence: full, partial, or limited. Under full independence, the student can work on any part of the course at any time. The only stipulation is that required assignments and assessments be completed by the end of the course. Under partial independence, the student must complete all required assignments and assessments in one block before he or she can move on to the next. Under limited independence, the instructor establishes a definite sequence of assignments and assessments. The student is limited in the choice of materials and/or sequence.

Regardless of the level of independence that the instructor selects, the program records all student selections of assignments and assessments for reference by both the instructor and the student.

Expanding Student Planning Capabilities. Through the use of a PLP, student planning can include term goals, student information profiles (student characteristics, expected outcomes, past performance, and so forth), and a carefully chosen academic program. The plan can track this information from the day a student enters the institution.

Long-Term Goals. Every student selects an academic program, but does this program match the student's long-term goals? Every student's personalized learning plan can begin with the student's long-term goals, assessed as the student enters the institution either through questionnaires or interviews. The goals provide a reference point against which the student can periodically check his or her progress and assess the direction that he or she is taking. If changes need to be made in these goals as the student matures, they can be easily entered into the computer. By maintaining an ongoing record of these long-term goals and the changes that occur, the computer constructs a history of the student. This history can provide insight for the student or those working with the student.

Technology-Based Multimedia Learning Resources. Personalized learning plans have a hand-in-glove relationship with technology-based multimedia learning resources. Access to a variety of media is essential for responding to individual learning modes and to reinforce the self-paced learning associated with PLPs.

Challenges for Institutional Researchers. Although the combination of PLPs with technology-based media in a transformed system offers the greatest potential for cost-effective learning, use of technology-based resources alone in a traditional educational environment can improve learning and reduce cost. However, complete systematic analysis of the cost-effectiveness of technology applications in traditional higher education taking all factors into account is not possible at this time. The differences in budget and cost accounting practices among institutions mean that we lack comparable and accurate cost data. Moreover, project accounting practices do not normally pay sufficient attention to support costs, such as occupancy and amortization of capital equipment investments, particularly in public institutions. In large part, these deficiencies result from the fact that cost containment is less important in institutions of higher education than improvement of learning. This stance is reflected in the policy at a number of institutions that technology will not replace faculty and in the resistance that faculty unions have shown to the introduction of technology. Finally, the absence of consensus on appropriate quantitative and qualitative measures of learning outcomes in both traditional and technology-based learning makes any evaluation of effectiveness difficult.

For these and other reasons, it is desirable to look at the learning outcomes and cost data associated with a spectrum of applications of technology to gain the broadest insights on how to plan for and achieve cost-effective results in the use of technology-based learning resources.

Military Services. Historically, military services have led efforts to apply technology in instruction. The report by Orlansky and String (1979) is regarded as a classic by those who have pioneered the utilization of computer-based instruction. Analyzing some thirty studies conducted after 1968, these authors concluded that computer-based instruction saves about 30 percent of the time needed under traditional instruction to complete the required courses. The time saved results in cost avoidance. Student achievement was found to be about the same as or greater than that with traditional instruction. This early evaluation provides a valuable reference point for the development of a perspective on the growing potential for cost-effective computer-based instruction as the cost of technology continues to decrease and performance increases.

A decade later, Fletcher (1990) reported that interactive videodisk instruction, applied in defense training and in the related settings of industrial training and higher education, improved achievement and was less costly than more conventional instruction. Routine use of this technology in defense training and education was recommended.

Business. The increased use of technology-based learning by companies has been fueled by the urgent need to reduce cost and improve performance in every part of the business, including employee education and training, in order to compete in world markets.

McDonald-Douglas (Lowenstein and Barbee, 1990) is using interactive videodisk delivery to train employees on a computer-aided design and drafting system. Students with videodisk training were more advanced than those who had been trained by traditional methods, and the per-student cost of training was lower. The cost of the training courseware and terminals for delivery was offset in sixteen months.

Steelcase, the world's largest manufacturer of office furniture, has implemented a technology-based learning system that makes employees responsible for their own learning. This system is one of the most complete self-directed interactive multimedia computer-based learning centers in the nation ("With the Learning Curve . . . ," 1991). Costs fell from $200 per learner under the traditional learning approach to $20.

IBM is currently using computer-based instruction to deliver 50 percent of its education and training. Substantial savings are being realized in both the cost of delivery and in employee time and travel. It is estimated that utilization will move to 75 percent by the end of the 1990s (Bowsher, 1989).

Higher Education. For companies, employee time and travel are major elements in the total cost of employee education and training, but the cost of student time and travel is not a direct responsibility of educational institutions. Nevertheless, such costs must be taken into account if higher education is to be responsive to student needs and if it is to operate in the most cost-effective manner. Technology can reduce time to graduation, which represents a cost saving for both student and institution. Decreasing cost of access saves the student money and increases enrollment for the institution.

Although it lags behind the military services and business, higher education is beginning to make significant use of technology in instruction. Boettcher (1992) describes the successful use of a wide range of technologies in many disciplines by higher education institutions of various sizes that serve a variety of student populations. The author based the determination of success on four criteria: First, the project improves student learning, and the link between learning improvement and technology investment is clear. Second, the project enriches curriculum and/or culture. Third, the project is generalizable. Fourth, the project hits or addresses targets of difficulty.

The author provides rough estimates of initial ongoing and replication costs in many cases. Although this information lacks uniformity and detail, it can be of help in planning cost-effective applications of technology.

One of the institutions that Boettcher (1992) studied is the University of Illinois at Urbana-Champaign (UIUC), which has twenty-five years of experience in the utilization of computer-based instruction (CBI) and interactive video learning. This utilization has increased learning and reduced laboratory costs. The instructional program and associated classroom management system have been implemented at approximately one hundred institutions.

Jones, Kane, Sherwood, and Avner (1983) report on an introductory classical mechanics course in an older UIUC program. To assess the impact of computer-based instruction, the same final exams were given to students taught in the usual way and to about the same number receiving computer-based instruction. The results showed that students in the CBI course did as well as those in the traditional course. The common final exam has been repeated periodically since the article was written, and the results are constant. The CBI course uses two-thirds as many teaching assistants as the traditional course per one hundred students taught, which results in savings. Moreover, data from twenty-four consecutive semesters show that students believe they learn more from the course in the interactive version than in the traditional lecture version.

The integrated curriculum in science, engineering, and mathematics at Rose-Hulman Institute of Technology exemplifies programs in which the use of technology enables faculty to move from teaching to coaching. In this curriculum, which emphasizes the formulation of problems and the interpretation of solutions, students use computer workstations and commercially available Mathematica software to explore broad themes that link science, engineering, and mathematics. The same number of faculty are involved as with the traditional program. A survey (Rogers, 1992) of faculty consistently rated students higher who had completed the integrated curriculum than a comparable group not in the integrated curriculum. Grade point averages were higher and attrition rates were lower for those in the integrated curriculum.

Commonality of Technology-Based Learning Resources. Although the cost of basic personal computers is decreasing rapidly—a trend that is likely to continue—it is not likely that the cost of creating courseware will follow the same pattern, at least in the near future. This situation is due in large part to the fact that academe demands much higher quality now than it did a few years ago. High quality is feasible with the increasingly advanced authoring systems, interactive multimedia, and other technologies now available, which all mean that the development process now requires more time and money. Current estimates of the cost to create one thirty-minute course incorporating the latest computer-based learning technologies are in the range of $40,000 to $50,000. Updating can average 10 to 20 percent annually of the initial cost.

Because of the sizable commitments of time and money involved, collaboration among institutions is essential if cost-effective courseware is to become widely available on a timely basis. Collaboration is necessary—first to arrive at a consensus on the content of the courseware to be developed, then to ensure wide usage, which reduces the risk attendant on the initial investment.

Technology-Based Distance Learning. Technology-based distance learning is widely used in the United States. A typical technology-based learning system provides communication between student and instructor by telephone, cable, or satellite; instruction is delivered by audio, interactive video, computer, or some combination of these technologies.

One essential element of a successful technology-based distance learning program is high-quality instructional materials, which require a much larger initial investment than the traditional lecture-based classroom course. To lower per-student cost, the course must be delivered to a large number of students. As just noted, it is desirable for institutions to collaborate in the development of technology-based course materials.

The literature contains many reports of studies on the cost-effectiveness of technology-based distance learning. Rule, DeWulf, and Stowitschek (1988) analyzed the cost of providing extensive in-service teacher training via interactive television to teachers in the classroom in three rural communities. They concluded that such training can be delivered simply and economically. A much more extensive technology-based distance learning program is under the aegis of the Community College of Maine (MacBrayne, 1992). In seventy-seven locations across Maine, students can choose from among forty-odd college courses, which are delivered via interactive television. This system has vastly increased accessibility to higher education in Maine without requiring the construction of a single new building. The $7.3 million cost of building the system is roughly the same as the cost of a new dormitory. True cost-effectiveness comparisons are not possible, because there is no feasible alternative in the locations where the program was implemented.

Because of the numerous considerations in determining cost-effectiveness of technology-based distance learning, AT&T has developed a model to assist institutions in designing the distance learning system most appropriate to their budget and needs (Chute and Balthazar, 1988). Another model for determining cost-effectiveness is provided by Markowitz (1987). His model includes a technique for determining the break-even point of a technology-based system, and it takes fixed and variable costs into account.

Continuous Quality Improvement. Total Quality Management (TQM) is a powerful unifying force in efforts to transform education, since it addresses every aspect of the institution, including leadership, administration, the classroom, and the curriculum (Chaffee and Sherr, 1992). TQM is not the answer but the process that can improve problem solving, improve education, and introduce creative and effective changes. High on the list of the hallmarks of total quality is continuous improvement. In fact, many educational institutions that have begun to focus on TQM principles have found that continuous quality improvement better describes their philosophy.

Gradual Implementation

Awareness is growing that collaboration is needed if there is to be a continuum from high school to college and from college to the world of work without serious interruption or unnecessary discontinuities in the learning experience. The critical ingredients are a personalized learning plan for lifelong learning; easy, low-cost access to technology-based learning materials; and increased student responsibility for learning. In a transforming education system, the role of faculty member changes from one of lecturer to facilitator of knowledge and learning. The inextricable relationship between that change and the student's assumption of increased responsibility for learning makes possible dramatic improvements both in productivity and in quality. Technology gives the instructor the opportunity to introduce concepts, problems, and learning opportunities that are not available in the classroom under the traditional lecture group instruction method. As a productivity tool, technology gives the individual faculty member the opportunity to concentrate on the vital human interaction in the areas of teaching where it is more important.

Realizing the full potential of the increased use of technology for achieving the improvements in productivity and quality that we so urgently need requires careful planning and incremental implementation of the transformation process.

A logical first step, even for an institution that faces budgeting constraints, is to establish a pilot program with selected groups of students. Such a program has virtually no risk. The pilot program provides each student with a personalized learning plan and emphasizes the maximum appropriate use of technology-based instruction and other transforming tools and processes. There is no magic formula for the number of students in the group. A reasonable pilot program might consist of two groups, each with one hundred students, in different academic programs. The cost of capital equipment and software would not exceed $25,000, and it could be less if computers were already available. It is critically important not to delay putting such a foundation into place or beginning the process of gaining the experience needed to plan and implement the wider use of technology wisely.

Collaboration with other institutions of higher education is critically important. The cost of assembling the necessary technology-based learning resources and the experience gained in applying all the transforming tools and processes are best shared. Progress with the pilot program will determine the rate at which the transforming process can be expanded to other areas.

B. Increased Use of Technology in Administration

Twenty-five years ago, use of computers was oriented toward the collection and sorting of data and the generation of reports from a central service on campus. This section describes developments in the administrative use of computers in four areas: student systems, business systems, recruiting, and fundraising.

Student systems began in the 1960s with arena-based registration and grade reporting. Curriculum, housing, student billing, and financial aid processing systems were added to this core. Integration of disparate student information functions began during the late 1970s, when centralized data bases were used to consolidate all facts about enrolled students. As the cost of new technology dropped, registration systems evolved into more sophisticated on-line or telephone access systems. Many other batch processing systems were also converted to on-line functions. In the early 1990s, this integrated student data base structure allowed such further improvements as automatic degree audit processing—a substitute for most routine academic advising. Simultaneously, faculty work load and classroom utilization statistics became readily available.

In the past, business systems, such as payroll and personnel processing, purchasing, financial systems, and inventory control, were designed for the requirements of a particular office or individual. The general assumption was that the office that collected particular data was also the end user or primary client for those data. Changes in reporting requirements and shrinking budget resources placed new demands on these systems. Data have been moved on-line. Systems have been redesigned to serve multiple clients across campus.

The number of college-bound seniors dropped nationwide in the late 1980s, a development that led institutions to use computer systems in their recruiting efforts. These systems included prospective applicant tracking tools, interfaces to testing services for transmission of standardized test scores, automatic response systems to generate letters to applicants, and a variety of on-line report functions for admissions officers. Automated admissions systems can process graduate students as well as undergraduates. Although these systems are focused on admissions, they have provided the beginnings of management information tools for institutional research. The profile of the incoming freshman class can be scrutinized for use in future recruiting efforts supporting important campus priorities, such as increasing cultural diversity.

Shrinking resources in the late 1980s and early 1990s increased the burden on campus fundraising efforts, particularly on public campuses, where state support has eroded. A natural evolution moved graduating students from the integrated student data base to an on-line alumni data base. Such systems also manage files on other prospective donors. Solicitations, acknowledgments, and general information about the university are automatically targeted in key segments of the alumni population.

Priorities for the Twenty-First Century. Strategic decisions on technology should focus on what is required in applications. Future priorities were predicted by MacDonald (in press). In the year 2000, students will arrive in campus residence halls and "dock" their computers in the campus network. The network will send welcoming messages to each student, review the courses for which he or she has registered remotely from off campus, present reading lists and course syllabi, and review the status of any outstanding financial obligations. Faculty in their offices will download messages from committees, students, and off-campus colleagues. These messages may include voice, video, text, and fax. Results of large research applications running on the network will be available, as will class homework assignments and graduate student applications awaiting review. For campus administrators, the network will provide easy access to all financial records.

The computer applications foreseen for the not too distant future suggest that scarce funds will tend to be directed toward decentralized systems and more sophisticated campus data networks. Access and delivery of information cannot be emphasized without an appropriate campus data network. Development of such a network has been cited as the number one priority for campus presidents (HEIRAlliance, 1992). The network must reach all academic and administrative areas on campus and guarantee links with the national and international networks commonly referred to as Internet. The cost of installing a complete data network can be substantial. However, in the absence of such links, the campus community is cut off from the vast resources now available across Internet. Acquiring this material in alternative forms, such as print media, delays availability and adds the cost of mailing, printing, and disposal. Lack of on-campus network connections (with associated file transfer and electronic mail capabilities) can result in inefficient duplicate data entry, queues at administrative offices, large staffs for paper transactions, and cumbersome processes for circulating memos and general information sharing.

Cost Reductions. Computer systems can be designed to reduce the number of administrative support staff who are required (MacDonald, in press). This design may require the reorganization of several administrative functions. Take, for example, the case in which several campus offices are collecting money from students in transactions involving cash, credit cards, or debit cards. Support staff are responsible for processing these payments and producing receipts. Each office may be using unique computer programs, even different computer systems. Computer applications can be designed to consolidate these functions under a single management. Use of automatic teller machines can make further staff reductions possible.

The use of computing technology presents an "opportunity to do more with less" (West, 1991, p. 3). The prospect is welcome, because it permits campuses to cope with increased administrative work loads and shrinking staff resources. Cost savings have been achieved by taking advantage of the economies of scale and centralized management in sharing of data networks, computer processors, and related software (Jeffery, 1992). While academic requirements must be the first priority on campus, choosing a computer architecture to meet academic needs that is also capable of administrative processing will hold down costs. The outsourcing of administrative computing is another way of reducing costs. However, short-term gains can mask the real long-term costs (Dué, 1992).

Institutional research can help a campus to understand the costs of technology. Typically, the costs of replacing manual operations by technology are not well understood. Thus, it is difficult to undertake cost-benefit analysis. When large transformations of administrative functions, such as the student information system or the alumni system, are undertaken, cost estimates from institutional research studies should be compared with the expenses of development, training, and future operation.

The burden of computing expense has shifted dramatically over the past seven years from hardware to software ("Making a Case for Software Management," 1993). The trend to smaller, more distributed processors has also influenced computing applications. However, distributed small machines increase the number of software licenses and hardware maintenance contracts required (Vinea, 1992). Ten years ago, commercial software might have been cheaper than in-house development. Today, build-or-buy decisions must weigh the cost of ongoing maintenance, particularly when application packages are required from commercial vendors. While computing services have had declining or level budgets over the last seven years, the combined cost of software purchases and software maintenance has risen by a factor of four; rapid increases have occurred since 1989 (MacDonald, in press). This trend has resulted in the cancellation of software licenses and in the reduction of choices among overlapping software packages. The cost of contractual software maintenance from commercial suppliers has increased by 10 to 15 percent.

Planning a software framework that is not tied to a particular vendor's hardware can maximize flexibility and reduce costs. For example, Standard Query Language (SQL) packages for extracting information from on-line data bases are available from many vendors. Individuals can use personal computers, advanced workstations, or mainframes to access the data base with a standard query tool. Even if the underlying data base structures change, the query language remains the same, a factor that minimizes conversion costs and the need for retraining.

Fortunately, the cost of computing hardware has dropped dramatically, a development that facilitates the deployment of such technology across campus. However, rapid technological changes are concurrently accelerating obsolescence. With careful analysis, new investments in technology can enhance the educational mission at minimal cost. The investment will pay off only if the plans provide for long-term operating costs, replacement of hardware and software, and training for new faculty and staff. New technology investments based on one-time capital funds prove to be expensive and to have few long-term benefits.

Capital investment in infrastructure—hardware, software, and network cable—will not bear fruit if the institution does not also have skilled professionals. Leadership for technology decisions should be vested in an experienced chief information officer with skills in computing technology and networking who reports to a senior vice president or the campus president. Assuring that professional staff within the technology organization have backgrounds in computer science, mathematics, economics, business, library science, and teaching is the key to success of such an operation.

Adequate provision of computing services requires not only an adequate number of support staff but also salaries that will attract qualified professionals. Staff members need ongoing professional development in order to update their capabilities.

To reap the maximum benefits from increasing the use of computer technology in administrative functions, a campus must not only handle the required day-to-day business transactions but provide a data resource that facilitates long-range planning and decision making. Institutional research can help to optimize these benefits. Early involvement in computing project cycles, with particular attention to the creation or addition of new data elements to the institutional data base, is necessary. According to Penrod and Dolence (1992, p. 23), a good data resource includes such features as "accessible summary information, longitudinal comparison data, and ad hoc retrieval and report generation capabilities."

Because administrative computing efforts are usually directed at administrative offices, they overlook many of the regular administrative functions performed by faculty. Aside from benefitting teaching and learning, computing resources can help to offset the effects of increasing class size. One example is the use of electronic mail for students and faculty in electronic study groups (MacDonald, in press). An electronic study group can share class discussion and follow up on related material without requiring individuals to be in the same place at the same time. Automated test scoring, electronic class lists, and on-line access to student records for advising represent other ways in which computing resources can increase faculty productivity.

Strategic alliances with other campus service providers can be essential for launching new initiatives. For example, any campus cable plan will involve the maintenance and facilities department, as will issues of deferred maintenance and renewal of facilities (MacDonald, in press). Baseline network standards should be established for new construction and remodeling. Standards are also necessary for between-building wiring, within-building wiring, offices and laboratories, on- and off-campus residence halls, and communications protocols. Campus networks can be developed incrementally as opportunities for laying cable arise. Short-term solutions can capitalize on existing copper wire until new funds become available.

Libraries are rapidly becoming the largest user of technology resources on campus. Increasing costs and fewer real dollars have changed acquisitions strategies at most libraries. As libraries look to network services to enhance their capabilities, the campus technology infrastructure becomes critical (MacDonald and Perry, 1991). Thus, computing services and libraries are forming another natural strategic alliance. Improved software tools and network access within the library benefit the entire campus community and require administrative planners to have a broad perspective.

Management information from well-planned computing systems will help senior administrators to make informed decisions. Comparisons are easy to make between many worthy high-priority projects. For example, classroom space is always critical, and it always seems insufficient. When automated room scheduling software is readily available, classrooms can be scheduled efficiently with minimal intervention. Such software improves the use of existing space and frees staff to perform other tasks. Good scheduling software also provides information on the number of students present on campus by hour and day. Such information makes it possible to improve campus management of transportation systems and parking spaces. A demand-analysis registration system is another type of critical management package. Employing demand analysis before students are assigned to class sections allows class sizes to be adjusted and sections to be added or closed. New sections can be added only to meet the most critical demand.

Concluding Thoughts. The use of technology in an institution should be part of the budget solution, not part of the problem. Some may argue that investment in technology is not warranted in times of reduced resources. To these voices I reply that investment should be guided by the answers to four questions: Will it provide access to new information? Will it reduce the amount of paper produced and filed? Will it reduce total cost? And will the resulting organization be more efficient? If the answers to these questions are positive, then innovative integration of technology into the administration of higher education will permit more to be done with less.

References

Boettcher, J. V. (ed.). *101 Success Stories of Information Technologies in Higher Education.* New York: McGraw-Hill, 1992.

Bowsher, J. "Interview." *Authorware Magazine,* Fourth Quarter 1989, pp. 15–17.

Chaffee, E. E., and Sherr, L. A. *Quality: Transforming Postsecondary Education.* ASHE-ERIC Higher Education Reports, no. 3. Washington, D.C.: Association for the Study of Higher Education, 1992.

Chute, A. G., and Balthazar, L. *An Overview of Research and Development Projects at the AT&T National Teletraining Center.* Cincinnati, Ohio: AT&T, 1988.

Dué, R. T. "The Real Costs of Outsourcing." *Information Systems Management,* 1992, 9 (1), 78–81.

Fletcher, J. D. *Effectiveness and Cost of Interactive Videodisk Instruction in Defense Training and Education.* IDA Paper P-2372. Alexandria, Va.: Institute for Defense Analysis, 1990.

Fletcher, J. D. *Individualized Systems of Instruction.* IDA Document D-1190. Alexandria, Va.: Institute for Defense Analysis, 1992.

HEIRAlliance. *What Presidents Need to Know . . . About the Integration of Information Technologies on Campus.* HEIRAlliance Executive Strategies Report No. 3. Boulder, Colo.: CAUSE, 1992.

Jeffery, B. "The New Role of Central MIS." *Computer Economic$ Report,* 1992, 14 (5), 1–3.

Jones, L. M., Kane, D., Sherwood, B. A., and Avner, R. A. "A Final Exam Comparison Involving Computer-Based Instruction." *American Journal of Physics,* 1983, 51 (6), 533–538.

Lowenstein, R., and Barbee, D. E. *The New Technology: Agent of Transformation.* Washington, D.C.: Government Printing Office, 1990.

MacBrayne, P. "Community College of Maine: A Statewide Associate Degree Program." In J. V. Boettcher (ed.), *101 Success Stories of Information Technologies in Higher Education.* New York: McGraw-Hill, 1992.

MacDonald, G. "Making Decisions with Shrinking Resources." In *Proceedings of the 1992 CAUSE National Conference*. Boulder, Colo.: CAUSE, in press.

MacDonald, G., and Perry, A. "Information Access, Computing Services, and Libraries: A Joint Offensive Team." In *Proceedings of the 1990 CAUSE National Conference*. Boulder, Colo.: CAUSE, 1991.

"Making a Case for Software Management." *Software Economics Letter*, Jan. 1993, pp. 5–6.

Markowitz, H., Jr. "Financial Decision Making: Calculating the Costs of Distance Education." *Distance Education*, 1987, *8* (2), 147–161.

N.E. Metro Technical College. *General Catalog, 1991–1993*. White Bear Lake, Minn.: N.E. Metro Technical College, 1992.

Orlansky, J., and String, J. *Cost-Effectiveness of Computer-Based Instruction in Military Training*. IDA Paper P-1375. Alexandria, Va.: Institute for Defense Analysis, 1979.

Penrod, J. I., and Dolence, M. G. *Reengineering: A Process for Transforming Higher Education*. CAUSE Professional Paper Series, no. 9. Boulder, Colo.: CAUSE, 1992.

Rickman, J. T., and Hubbard, P. L. *The Electronic Campus*. Maryville, Mo.: Prescott, 1992.

Rogers, G. M. *The First-Year Curriculum in Science, Engineering, and Mathematics: The Sophomore Year Experience*. Terre Haute, Ind.: Rose Hulman Institute of Technology, 1992.

Rule, S., DeWulf, M., and Stowitschek, J. "An Economic Analysis of In-Service Teacher Training." *American Journal of Distance Education*, 1988, *2* (2), 12–22.

Vinea, V. "Preparing for a Distributed Environment." *Information Systems Management*, 1992, *9* (2), 79–81.

West, T. W. "Being Lean and Meaningful in the 1990's." *Cause/Effect*, 1991, *14* (3), 3–5.

"With the Learning Curve, Steelcase Hopes to Become a Learning-Based Company in the 1990's." *Authorware Magazine*, Second Quarter 1991, pp. 4–9.

WILLIAM C. NORRIS, author of Part A, is chair of the William C. Norris Institute in Bloomington, Minnesota, and founder and chair emeritus of Control Data Corporation.

GERALDINE MACDONALD, author of Part B, is associate vice president for computing services at the State University of New York, Binghamton.

Small increases in R&D funding and the state of the economy pose serious challenges to research universities. It is unlikely that the financial pressures on these institutions will moderate in the future. Research universities will be challenged to downsize without compromising their quality.

Research Universities Face Difficult Choices

Joseph Froomkin

More than 90 percent of the nation's academic research and development is concentrated in a mere hundred of the roughly three thousand establishments that offer higher education degrees (National Science Foundation, 1991). Each of these hundred institutions has areas of excellence, but many do not aspire to complete coverage of all fields, and some specialize in applied areas, most notably agriculture. A small number of institutions, perhaps thirty or forty, can be considered research-intensive universities on the basis of the extent to which they devote their effort and resources to the advancement of knowledge. Lately, the distinction between research-intensive and other types of universities has become increasingly difficult to make because a substantial volume of pathbreaking investigations is now conducted in these other types of institutions.

A university administrator or trustee in a research-intensive institution views additions to knowledge as a badge of honor, one of the principal reasons for the institution's existence. Nobel prizes, National Academy of Science memberships, and other awards to the faculty are highly valued. In contrast, instruction, especially of undergraduates, may receive only lip service. Resources for teaching are likely to be cut first when sacrifices have to be made. Many state-financed institutions, especially the large ones, tend to discharge the undergraduate-teaching function on the cheap. Despite the nearly universal lack of attention to undergraduates, research-intensive universities continue to attract above-average students in both their undergraduate and graduate programs.

NEW DIRECTIONS FOR INSTITUTIONAL RESEARCH, no. 79, Fall 1993 © Jossey-Bass Publishers

Recent Challenges and the Response of Research Universities

Undergraduate Program. The support that research universities will receive in the future depends increasingly on the loyalty of their undergraduates. During the past decade, alumni contributed a significant amount of money to build up the endowments of leading public and private institutions. Most significant contributors to the fund drives were former undergraduates who attended these schools prior to 1955.

It is likely that these institutions have missed out on the opportunity of producing a whole generation of loyal undergraduates. The riots during the late 1960s were a symptom of students' dissatisfaction with the institutions that they attended. Curriculum reforms that addressed past dissatisfaction laid the ground for the alienation of future generations. In the humanities, reforms focused on the scope of introductory courses: Should they be limited to traditional discussion of Western culture, or should the curriculum be broadened to acquaint students with texts that inform thinking in other parts of the world? Another more fundamental dichotomy deals with the purpose of introductory courses. Should it be to expose students to information about important topics (the so-called knowledge worth having), or should the courses be oriented to helping students think, examine systematically, and be capable, as Thomas Jefferson puts it in words inscribed on his monument in Washington, D.C., of debating issues "as new discoveries are made, new truths discovered, and manners and opinions change with change in circumstances"? The absence of consensus has weakened the moral prestige of our leading institutions in the halls of Congress. It has also resulted in instruction that does little to force undergraduates to reason systematically.

Economies at the expense of undergraduates appear to have been especially deleterious in the teaching of undergraduate science to nonscience majors. Undergraduate programs for majors were revised in the 1960s and 1970s to make them more rigorous, as departments vied with each other to train students to be successful applicants for graduate school. The increased effort demanded from students concentrating on a major caused departments to pay less attention to other students. The innovative solution was to introduce two streams of courses, a demanding one for majors and an undemanding, watered-down one for the rest. Financial constraints are at the root of the debased curriculum: Science labs are expensive.

This trend is extremely dangerous because research-intensive universities attract the most gifted students, and many important corporate jobs in private industry and a high proportion of appointees in the executive branch of government are filled by graduates from these schools. Executives and policymakers are likely to come from the ranks of students who do not continue their graduate education in a science-oriented discipline but opt for a professional school, such as business or law. It is important for them to be well enough grounded in both hard and social science to keep up with developments in knowledge that could affect the well-being of this country. The watered-down courses offered for nonmajors are not likely to provide future leaders with the knowledge that they need. The recipients of bachelor's degrees from research universities who opt for professional schools could suffer in comparison to graduates of smaller liberal arts colleges that retain relatively fundamental programs for the teaching of science. Alumni who feel that their education put a brake on their success are likely to contribute less to their schools (J. Froomkin, 1983).

Graduate Program. The potential problems of graduate education dwarf those of the undergraduate curriculum. In the past decade, the program for the Ph.D.—a research degree—has become much more rigorous, a euphemism for *more specialized*, at least in research universities. The preferred outcome for the recipients of these degrees is a position that involves both research and teaching. The imbalance between the production of doctorates at research universities and faculty openings was already felt during the 1980s. The current downward pressure on resources will accentuate it.

During the past two decades, roughly half of all recipients of the doctorate found work in administrative jobs at nonprofit institutions or in mundane and applied research in the private sector. Competition from Eastern Europe and the former Soviet Union will jeopardize many of these positions. Nearly one hundred thousand scientists with the equivalent of American doctorates will be looking for jobs at a fraction of the pay that their local counterparts have come to expect. A number of computer companies have already established computer groups in the East to work at the minimum American wage or less. In the future, it is conceivable that a significant portion of all research will be exported to that part of the world (Markoff, 1992).

Competition from the East will be felt most acutely because of cuts anticipated in the portion of the military budget that deals with atomic weapons. Thousands of persons with advanced degrees in the United States and abroad will have to find new jobs in other fields.

Even in a field like biotechnology, where the United States is preeminent and Eastern European countries are lagging, a change in emphasis from identifying genes to understanding how they function may benefit the East. The complex mathematics of the influence that genes have on proteins may favor research by the strong mathematical scientists in the former Soviet Union. The move to export high-level jobs may rival the exodus of assembly jobs in electronics and disappoint those who hope that the United States can regain its lead in high technology.

Twenty-five years ago I was the only social scientist to warn that the production of doctorates was likely to stabilize. The consensus forecast was that it would double (Wolfle and Kidd, 1991, p. 786). Today, I can echo the federal assistant secretary for higher education in warning that the production of doctorates in the United States will have to be reduced dramatically. In all probability, the reduction may have to be as much as 30 to 50 percent below present levels. A wrenching decision will have to be made whether to cut out programs in research universities or elsewhere (Reid-Wallace, 1992).

What Happened to Resources

Historical Perspective. At his inauguration in October 1992, Jack W. Peltason, the new president of the University of California system, declared that "never during the one-hundred-and-twenty-five-year history of the university has it been stronger. . . . At the same time, perhaps never has it been in greater peril" (D. Froomkin, 1992, p. A3). The research universities, the crown jewels of the postsecondary establishment, are facing the greatest challenge of any of the institutions in the postsecondary sector. The United States has nurtured them on a large scale for only forty or fifty years, and it is possible that they may wilt.

Starting with modest beginnings in the 1930s, the postsecondary system blossomed, so that by the beginning of the 1970s, the claim that the university system in the United States was second to none was unlikely to be disputed anywhere in the Western world. The rain of Nobel prizes, the prominence of American social science, and the increasing sophistication of our contribution to the humanities justified self-congratulation.

Much of this success was due to the generous funding of research. Research expenditures' share of the national product increased by a factor of three between 1950 and 1970. By contrast, grants for research increased only slightly faster than the gross national product in the course of the past twenty years. As a result, the production of persons with doctorates outran the demand in university research settings.

Even more than resentment over student protests, this overproduction of persons with advanced degrees contributed to a decline in sympathy for the special needs of research-intensive universities, both public and private. The notion gained wide acceptance that general support and federal research funds should be spread among a large number of campuses.

As the cost of research escalated, especially in the biological sciences, the presidents of leading research institutions became increasingly resentful of the federal policy of spreading research funds among many institutions. State legislatures exacerbated financial problems by equalizing support between institutions. Most leading public institutions, which until the mid 1970s were increasing their share of the state higher education dollar, maintained but did not widen the advantage that they had gained in the two preceding decades (J. Froomkin, 1990). The federal government, which provides two-thirds of noninstitutional research and development resources that universities receive, still concentrates its aid on a few institutions. Currently, it allocates 50 percent of its money to thirty institutions, as contrasted to three-quarters of the smaller sum that it distributed in 1950.

The realization that conditions had changed drastically hit the research-intensive community in the 1980s. During the recession of 1982, a decline in state revenues caused a number of states to introduce stringent economies. This time, the flagship schools, which had escaped the impact of previous cost reduction drives, were not spared. Especially in the rust belt, such high-status schools as the University of Michigan suffered severely from cuts. Private universities, which depended only peripherally on state appropriations, also felt the effect of the slowdown in economic activity during that and subsequent years. Since their net receipts from tuition—that is, tuition less scholarship aid—appear to be tied to the growth of incomes, their increases were constrained by the anemic performance of the economy.

The Past Ten Years. The economic dip in the early 1980s was followed by a decade of slow growth. The postsecondary establishment acutely felt its effect. Overall, research universities managed to increase the real remuneration of their faculty but in a very small way. According to Getz and Siegfried (1991, p. 376), faculties at research institutions registered gains of 2.33 percent a year, a figure that compares favorably with the 2.10 percent a year noted for all postsecondary institutions. The number of new hires also increased slightly faster than the average, despite the fact that the number of graduate students declined. The financial reports of individual universities suggest that most of the increase in instructional dollars per student was due to the growing number of administrators and to some increases in the cost of fringe benefits, not to an effort to put more resources into instruction.

For the first time in thirty years, research-intensive universities were faced with the necessity of making choices between disciplines that promised to deliver significant payoffs for increased investment in research and older, traditional endeavors, including some in which the economy no longer required as many persons with advanced degrees.

The choices are especially difficult in such fields as physics, where research opportunities in some subfields seem to be increasingly less promising, and in some of the more conventional areas of biological research, which explorations of the structure of the human genome are rendering obsolete or not cost-effective. In the humanities, the waning fashion of deconstruction is threatening the relevance of some research, and in the social sciences, the leading edge of sociological research is approaching the methodology of research in economics, a development that makes the more conventional sociological investigation appear irrelevant.

The problem that all postsecondary institutions face is that they are highly labor-intensive, and in the long run their costs outrun increases in the cost of living, since the pay of employees in academia must roughly follow trends in wages in the rest of the economy. As long as there are no dramatic breakthroughs in productivity in teaching, where human contact between student and professor is still considered important, at least at the graduate level, and as long as we have no accepted measure for the assessment of productivity in research, allocations as a fixed percentage of the national product will put more serious pressure on research-oriented schools to save money. According to some university administrators, the need to effect drastic economies is reaching crisis proportions in the limping economy of the 1990s. The crisis is particularly acute in states—most notably California—that have not had to cut allocations to higher education in the past.

Brighter Future or Tougher Options?

A return to full employment and a more prosperous economy may alleviate some of the financial crisis in higher education, but the general consensus is that the penury will not disappear. The President's Council of Advisors on Science and Technology concluded in December 1992 that research-intensive universities should adopt selective strategies to scale down their activities in an environment of limited resources. These were among the suggestions made by a committee sympathetic to the needs of research universities (its vice chairman and the reputed author of the suggestions was Harold Shapiro, president of Princeton University): Eliminate or downsize some departments and specialties rather than sustain less than world-class activities in every area of science and engineering. Collaborate with other academic, industrial, and governmental institutions in sharing instructional and research facilities. Start new programs and build new facilities only when the resources needed to sustain them can be identified for a long period of time. Develop permanent institutional mechanisms for strategic planning that will foster a balance between activities and resources (President's Council of Advisors on Science and Technology, 1992).

The report says nothing about the organization needed to implement the strategic planning or about the mechanism by which an institution can project the likely balance of needs and resources. This reticence is due to the difficulty of generalizing about the policy changes that research universities may implement. Each institution is organized in its own way and has a tradition that it treasures. Some universities, most notably Harvard, are extremely decentralized, with each school responsible for its own budget. Other institutions, such as Princeton, do not grant subsets of the university the kind of autonomy that Harvard does. Yet, in practically all cases, they are faculty, rather than administrators, who set policy and have a preponderant influence on the level of budgets. Hence, most leading research institutions prefer vigorous steps aimed at increasing their revenues to restructuring.

Higher Tuition? One of the first items that institutions tap to increase for revenue is tuition. Public institutions, which charge a mere fraction of the tuition and fees that prevail in the private sector, raised tuitions in 1990 and 1991 to offset part of the shortfall in state subsidies. The increases, from a relatively low level, were especially steep in California, and they were justified as necessary to keep teaching salaries competitive (D. Froomkin, 1992). The public outcry will determine whether this trend continues, because state subsidies for public schools may not be restored to past levels when prosperity returns.

Private institutions have less leeway to increase tuition. In the long run, tuition at the leading research universities is roughly equal to the average per capita income, and it is likely to rise only in concert with this variable (J. Froomkin, 1990).

The popularity of college aid programs will probably inspire Congress to raise the ceiling on Pell grants, which will reduce the impact of tuition increases on some of the poorer students; it may also encourage further increases in tuition and fees. In the final analysis, tuition increases are not likely to solve the financial problems of institutions, either public or private. At best, tuition finances less than half of the outlays (net of hospital receipts and expenditures for schools that have associated hospitals) in private research-oriented universities. Most administrators in these schools are reluctant to increase undergraduate tuition drastically despite the fact that applications to these schools exceed the number of available freshmen places. They are afraid that drastic increases will discourage gifted but less wealthy students from applying and will force the schools to revert to their pre–World War II role as enclaves of privileged but not necessarily gifted students. In the public sector, tuition provides a modest fifth or sixth of instructional outlays, but it may rise to one quarter during this decade.

More from Gifts and Endowments? The silver lining in the cloud hanging over the financial prospects of research-intensive universities is revenue from endowment. In the private sector, the net value of these endowments roughly trebled during the past ten years (Andersen, 1991). The lion's share, close to $20 billion in 1990, is concentrated at some twenty private research-intensive universities. A number of research-intensive public universities have smaller but still impressive endowments.

However, the silver lining has tarnished recently. The growth rate of endowments—a combination of income and appreciation—appears to have declined precipitously. When rates of interest were high and the stock and realty markets were booming, as they were in the mid 1980s, increases of 25 to 30 percent a year were not unusual. Later in the decade, when interest rates declined, the increase in the value of fixed income parts of university portfolios compensated for the decline in income. The latest, scattered financial reports of research-intensive universities indicate that the endowments are increasing at single-digit rates, with some growing only 5 or 6 percent a year. This slow growth has dashed hopes that a much higher proportion of endowments could be contributed to the operating expenses of private schools.

Research-intensive universities in the public sector have much rosier prospects for financing an increasing proportion of their outlays with private gifts and income from growing endowments. Necessity is the mother of fundraising, and a number of leading public institutions have had substantial success.

In contrast, some private institutions have reached a ceiling on their fundraising. Thus, the champion fundraiser of them all, Harvard, recently reduced the goal of its fund drive by a third to a still impressive $2 billion. In private universities that are heavily endowed and that have rich and loyal alumni, endowment funds and gifts account for some 15 percent of their operating outlays (once again net of hospital receipts). In contrast, the public institutions, latecomers in the outside support game, cannot count on receiving more than 5 or 6 percent of their budget from outside funds. Moreover, if institutions do not take care to segregate (or hide) these funds to serve objectives that state legislatures have not sanctioned, the advantage that research-oriented universities have in appropriations may be eliminated by jealous representatives from districts where institutions have lower prestige and less support per student.

Research and Development. The importance in the budget of research and development is the sine qua non that distinguishes research-intensive universities from other institutions in the postsecondary sector. The principal source of outside funds in this field is the federal government, which in 1990 provided roughly three out of every four research dollars. The proportion is slightly higher in private institutions and lower in research-intensive state schools that have expertise in agricultural research subsidized by state government.

State and local governments and private industry each contributed slightly under 10 percent of the total, and other sources, mostly philanthropy, contributed the remaining 8 percent. Looking at past trends in these shares, one is impressed with the constancy, overall, of the federal government's role. Funds from other sources, especially industry, increased faster than federal resources, yet they continue to play a relatively modest part in the financing of academic R&D.

Industry, which provided some 11 percent of research and development funds in 1990, funneled its moneys mostly to schools with strong engineering departments (National Science Foundation, 1991, p. 25). Since nearly 50 percent of all research and development funds received in academic environments during the past decade was spent on biological and medical fields, one could reasonably expect that more private sector support would be directed to this end. There is considerable controversy about the reasons for industry's failure to support medical research by universities. One reason often mentioned is that biotechnology research is not yet close to delivering commercial products. Another, more likely reason is that scientists have become much more sophisticated financially, and, as soon as they are on the verge of a practical application, they spin off practical endeavors to a private venture.

Research-oriented universities are not organized to profit from the scientific breakthroughs that take place within their walls. The tradition of openness in the communication of research results—a tradition that some researchers claim is being eroded by scientists who hope to make a financial killing—is an important part of the atmosphere of cutting edge research. Alliances with commercial firms that give them first access to research and that require results to remain unpublished for some time are inimical to the traditions of most first-rate universities. For a substantial proportion of the very best scientists, the prospect of a Nobel prize is more attractive than millions from a Wall Street–inspired spin-off. Nevertheless, some scientists appear to have succumbed to the lure of big money.

The hope of a marriage between research universities and business, in which research universities sponsor and become partners in promising start-ups, received some attention as a result of a suggestion from Jack W. Peltason, president of the University of California System. He asked that in order to fund such start-ups the university system be allowed to retain $4 million in royalty payments now turned over to the state. University of California officials were quoted as saying that the resulting activity could contribute as much as $9.5 billion to the state's economy (Lively, 1993).

Knowledgeable observers of university activity in the private sector, most notably those at the Massachusetts Institute of Technology (MIT), were unenthusiastic about the future of such arrangements. MIT is probably the leader in producing usable inventions, and its experience, which resulted in the spin-off of its research and engineering arm as the MITRE Corporation, gives particular weight to their skepticism.

Restructuring Resources. The financial stringency affecting research-intensive universities is likely to persist even if they increase their revenues and the U.S. economy returns to full employment. There are two reasons for this pessimistic prognosis: First, during a period of prosperity, the pressure to increase the wages of faculty will wipe out all the small incremental increases that may benefit the higher education sector. Second, advances in science, new breakthroughs, and new fashions will require the research effort of the leading institutions to be refocused continuously. Until recently, refocusing meant that new activities were added to existing lines of research. In the future, as the presidential panel cited earlier has advised, activities that do not attain world-class status should be abandoned. Most administrators and faculties are reluctant to make such decisions. It is inconceivable to them that their institutions cannot lead in a newly developed field if only the necessary resources are found to build a nucleus of brilliant researchers.

What appeared to be a promising suggestion to this end—recruiting part-time or temporary help from the business sector—is not meeting with much success. Proposals that the best of the private sector researchers be involved in or lent to universities are more often advanced than implemented. This lack of success has two explanations: differences in culture between even the least product-oriented industrial lab and the university and the reluctance of firms in the private sector to allow research leaders to leave their research facilities, a reluctance that the recent decline in profits experienced by many large firms with important research commitments has reinforced. In February 1993, IBM, a true believer in fundamental research, cut its budget by 15 percent and pledged to reorient research to more practical fields that would be of less interest to the leading research universities.

Past experience in attempts to apply management principles to the running of prestigious universities forces us to conclude that these institutions are sui generis. In many instances, faculty revolts stopped administration plans for the retrenchment of marginal departments or schools. Some universities have attempted to cut costs by classifying their faculty into productive researchers and drones. The drones were scheduled for more contact hours with students. The unanticipated or possibly unstated ancillary benefit of this policy was that some expensive senior faculty members resigned. Efforts to introduce similar policies at some of our leading institutions were checkmated on several occasions. Such measures were proposed at some private Ivy League schools but did not make it through the faculty senate.

Are Research-Intensive Institutions in Danger?

If the problems mount fast and changes are implemented slowly, some of the existing research-intensive universities may lose their leadership role. They face two sets of challenges. One set of challenges comes from up-and-coming states, such as Texas, which has plans for expanding the medical school in Dallas and for creating an entirely new research park in the vicinity of San Antonio (Culliton, 1992). The gains of such institutions come at the expense of former leaders.

An even more important challenge to the concentrated nature of research and instruction in the United States may come from technological developments. Donald N. Langenberg (1992, pp. 5–6), chancellor of the University of Maryland, remarked that technology has made it possible to sit "at home before a PC and [work] with a veritable cornucopia of networked information and communications resources." Mainframes, the dominant source of processing information in the past, now serve networks, and it does not matter to the user whether they are next door or half a continent away. Langenberg (1992, p. 6) believes that "a growing proportion of our . . . population . . . will find their needs served by a . . . delocalized higher educational system . . . made possible by a delocalized national information system." It is likely that the information revolution will also affect research. In the past, the community of scholars and students was of necessity centered around a library. As an increasing proportion of library materials becomes accessible through computers, the location of research is likely to be affected drastically.

Communication between scholars in a given field is now more often served by the facsimile machine than by propinquity or the camaraderie of the commons room. One hears increasingly that outstanding research, especially in the pure sciences, is being done in unlikely places. Many of the best younger researchers trained by leading scientists in the famous universities are employed elsewhere. The new generation that is working in the provinces may be currently offering equally good, or even better, training to assistants, doctoral and postdoctoral students, than they can receive in the large labs of leading research universities, which may be sloppily supervised by aging stars.

Modern technology is also threatening the rationale for the German type of university, which organizes research and training under a single authority. The recent controversy about overhead rates may speed the establishment of autonomous science centers, some university centered, others organized on the pattern of national laboratories in France or the United States. How this will affect the reputed symbiotic relationship between teaching and research needs critical attention.

The recently appointed presidents of Harvard, Columbia, and Chicago were all expected to find new solutions to the financial problems of their institutions, not just increasingly energetic fundraising. Faculties at those institutions were hoping that the new leadership would create a consensus that could operate the institutions with less money but without the loss of comity. This is possible. In a few instances of controlling budgets, most notably in Princeton, the personality and tact of the institution's president or chancellor appear to have been successful in catalyzing a shift of resources within the university. Most likely the new presidents will follow the path of the administrators who have been successful in the past and take small, incremental steps to effectuate savings. They will disband small departments that have little political clout. They may nibble at the peripheral activities of existing research programs and departments. In all cases, the cuts will be discussed at great length with faculty leaders, and a consensus will be established.

Despite their problems and shortcomings, leading research universities are still hothouses for the intellectual development of gifted undergraduate and graduate students, places where young people infect each other with enthusiasm. The survival of the research universities depends on their ability to become leaner, but conventional cost cutting could destroy their spirit.

References

Andersen, C. J. "Endowments: How Big and Where?" *Research Briefs*, 1991, 2, 6.

Culliton, B. C. "Optimistic, Independent, Aggressive: Texas Shoots for the Top in Science." *Nature*, 1992, 357, 623–624.

Froomkin, D. "UC Chief Inaugurated amid Protest." *Orange County Register*, October 17, 1992, p. A3.

Froomkin, J. "The Research Universities." In J. Froomkin (ed.), *Crisis in Higher Education*. New York: Academy of Political Science, 1983.

Froomkin, J. "The Impact of Changing Levels of Financial Resources on the Structure of Colleges and Universities." In S. A. Hoenack and E. L. Collins (eds.), *The Economics of American Universities*. Albany: State University of New York Press, 1990.

Getz, M., and Siegfried, J. J. "Costs per Student over Time." In C. T. Clotfelter and others (eds.), *Economic Challenges in Higher Education*. Chicago: University of Chicago Press, 1991.

Langenberg, D. N. "Statement to the President's Council of Advisors on Science and Technology." July 24, 1992.

Lively, K. "U. of California Plans Company to Push Inventions." *Chronicle of Higher Education*, Jan. 20, 1993, pp. A21, A25.

Markoff, J. "U.S. Lead in Software Faces a Rising Threat." *New York Times*, Oct. 25, 1992, p. E16.

National Science Foundation. *Selected Data on Academic Science and Engineering R&D Expenditures: FY 1990*. Washington, D.C.: National Science Foundation, 1991.

President's Council of Advisors on Science and Technology. *Renewing the Promise: Research-Intensive Universities and the Nation*. Washington, D.C.: Government Printing Office, 1992.

Reid-Wallace, C. "Is Higher Education Ready for the Twenty-First Century?" *George Washington University Magazine*, 1992, *3* (1), 29–30.

Wolfle, D., and Kidd, C. V. "The Future Market for Ph.D.'s." *Science*, 1991, *173*, 784–793.

JOSEPH FROOMKIN, an economic consultant, was assistant commissioner for planning and evaluation in the U.S. Office of Education (1966–1969) and director of the Policy Research Center for Higher Education (1976–1983).

The institutional research office facilitates the decision-making process by developing information and analysis, identifying options, and maintaining a forward view.

Facilitating Decisions Under Scarcity

Stefan D. Bloomfield

To cope with scarcity, an organization must decide on the most effective use of its limited resources. Such decisions often involve difficult and emotion-laden choices among otherwise worthwhile institutional endeavors. Yet the bottom line remains unchanged: Net total expenses must be brought into balance with the level of resources available. For institutions of higher education, cost reduction strategies span the gamut from across-the-board cuts uniformly imposed on each institutional unit to highly selective cuts (sometimes termed the *deep-and-narrow strategy*) imposed on targeted instructional programs or support activities.

The strategies that an institution selects to cope with scarcity may reflect the management style of its president, may be determined by a highly participative campuswide process, or may be dictated simply by the magnitude of the fiscal crisis. No matter what the decision process, the resulting distribution of budget cuts and reallocation of resources will have been intended to accomplish some combination of purposes. The college or university's institutional research office can and should assist in the identification of such intended purposes and in the analysis of possible means of accomplishing them. This chapter discusses the conceptual decision-making framework within which an institutional research office should be prepared to function.

Understanding the Context

The ultimate response of a college or university to conditions of scarcity will be shaped by both the context in which scarcity occurs and the conditions under which the decisions must be made. Successful analysis and decision making require explicit identification and widespread understanding of these factors. A first obligation of an institutional research office, therefore, is to help administration and faculty appreciate the scope of the problem.

Magnitude of Scarcity. The critical dimensions characterizing the context of scarcity include the magnitude and duration of the fiscal stress and the political agenda that drives the situation or constrains the solutions. The impetus for decision making commonly derives from a realization of the magnitude of the scarcity—the reduced budget within which the institution will be forced to operate. Unfortunately, as readers of the *Chronicle of Higher Education* are well aware, the magnitude of scarcity at many institutions has become a moving target. Colleges and universities have made enormous analytical and administrative efforts to meet specified budgetary goals only to be faced with new fiscal challenges as economic conditions have deteriorated or political policies have shifted. The result for many institutions has been a continuing series of cutback decisions and coping strategies, which almost inevitably leave the organization in a less advantageous position than if the full magnitude of the necessary cutback had been known from the beginning. To the extent to which careful study of economic trends and political currents can foresee such incremental cutbacks, the decision-making process can be increasingly effective. Colleges and universities with active and systematic environmental scanning programs should be better positioned to base their decision making on ultimate levels of scarcity (Keller, 1983).

Duration of Scarcity. Effective environmental scanning can also improve an institution's understanding of the likely duration of scarcity. If colleges and universities have shown evidence of any common myopia in this decade, it is in the belief that conditions of scarcity will be short-lived. The widespread faith that society will reaffirm the intrinsic value of higher education and that funding will ultimately (and relatively quickly) be restored to former levels has relentlessly driven campuses to shortsighted decision making. Budget reductions of convenience and across-the-board cutback strategies are seen everywhere. These strategies would be quite appropriate if the scarcity proved to be short-lived. However, such ride-out-the-storm strategies can critically weaken colleges and universities faced with a long-term financial challenge.

Political Considerations. Scarcity may result from changes in global or local economic conditions, from emerging demographic trends, or from the pursuit of particular political agendas by external entities. When fiscal pressures reflect a political agenda, the selection of decision-making alternatives may be constrained in additional ways. Not only the range of decision alternatives but the process of decision making itself must often be modified to reflect underlying political considerations: Rational analysis must share the stage with political maneuvering, and open communication must be compromised by discretion.

Deadlines. Another contextual characteristic that must be identified and understood is the time frame within which decisions must be implemented.

Commonly, budget reduction deadlines do not allow sufficient time for careful analysis or deliberate discussion. Clearly, the process adopted must conform to the time available. It is all the more critical, therefore, for institutional research staff to be adequately prepared before the decision process begins: in this case, to have already instituted a systematic program of environmental scanning that will allow the college or university to understand the likely magnitude, duration, and political context of scarcity before the decision making must occur.

Knowing the Institution's Purpose

It seems almost a cliché: To cope with scarcity successfully, an institution must have a sense of where it is going (Bowen and Glenny, 1980; Chaffee, 1984). The college or university must know why it exists and have a clear picture of how it might evolve the better to fulfill its mission. The literature on mission statements is voluminous; see Lang and Lopers-Sweetman (1991) for a comprehensive bibliography on this subject. A clear consensus emerges from these writings: The mission statements of institutions of higher education tend to be indistinguishable. Most are too general or abstract to provide a compelling rationale for the institution's existence, and most do not help the reader understand how the institution could evolve the better to fulfill that mission (Davies, 1986).

Vision Statements. To address this problem, some colleges and universities have elaborated on their mission statements in accompanying vision statements. If a mission statement is understood to articulate the institution's reason for existence, the vision statement fleshes out this abstraction by describing what the institution and its academic community will be like at some future date when the mission is more fully realized. The credibility of the vision statement depends not only on its faithfulness to the statement of mission but also on its attainability—the confidence it engenders that we can get there from here. By anchoring its aspirations in the institution's current status and by taking likely developments in the external environment into account, the vision statement can describe a preferred and attainable end state.

In effect, the vision statement articulates a set of goals as institutional characteristics to be pursued. Insisting that such characteristics be observable and measurable allows readers of the vision statement to endow ideals expressed in the mission statement with concrete substance. For example, the mission statement of Oregon State University (1992, p. 1) reads in part, "Oregon State University serves the people of Oregon, the nation, and the world through education, research, and service . . . Oregon State has an inherent commitment to provide a comprehensive array of high-quality educational programs in the sciences, liberal arts, and selected professions . . . As a Land Grant and Sea Grant university, Oregon State has a special responsibility for education and research enabling the people of Oregon and the world to develop and utilize human, land, atmospheric, and ocean resources." The vision statement for Oregon State University (1992, p. 2), which is based on the mission statement and which incorporates forecasts of the institution's internal and external environments, reads in part:

> In the year 2000 . . . the majority of Oregon State University students will be undergraduates who seek general education and/or preparation for the professions. To serve both our students and our society, Oregon State University will develop more flexible majors that integrate knowledge and skills from traditionally separate disciplines. There will be increasing emphasis on multidisciplinary programs and the associated synthesis and integration of knowledge. In response to the complex and changing nature of the professions, education will be designed to prepare an informed and caring citizenry and to insure technical competence. To this end, the professional programs will become increasingly linked in educationally sound, innovative ways to each other and to the liberal arts and sciences.

The next step is crucial, for it forces the college or the university to explore the implications of the vision statement for the specific structure and operation of the existing institution. Such implications commonly describe an institution that differs from the one that presently exists: The organizational and academic structure, the emphasis and priority accorded various programs, and the mix of students can all differ. These expressed differences combine to establish a sense of direction for the college or university, a direction rooted in the mission statement and shaped by the internal and external forces that provide the context for the future.

We could draw the following implications from Oregon State's vision statement: Oregon State University's instructional and research programs will be shaped by a primary substantive focus on natural resources and the physical environment, with particular concern for implications for human development. Programs in the liberal arts, sciences and applied sciences that are unusually expensive and that do not reinforce such a focus will be redirected, reduced in scope, or eliminated. Oregon State University's tradition of interdepartmental cooperation will be protected and enhanced in support of increasingly important interdisciplinary instructional and research programs.

By accepting the vision statement and its implications, the academic community acknowledges that physical, organizational, and programmatic changes and resource shifts can be desirable for the institution, whether or not they are prompted by conditions of scarcity. This, more than anything else, is the key to coping successfully with scarcity: campuswide understanding and acknowledgment that the institution is destined to evolve, campuswide support for the direction of evolution expressed in the vision statement, and campuswide confidence that the institution's leaders will use all available resource reallocation opportunities, including cutbacks, to progress toward the vision.

Leadership Challenge. One of the toughest challenges that leaders must face in this approach to scarcity is obtaining campuswide consensus on a vision statement once its implications have been understood. Embedded in the notion of change is the shifting of priorities, usually reflected in a reallocation of resources. Inevitably, the vision statement will give rise to perceptions by faculty and students of winners and losers among the institution's programs. Heated campus debate is almost inevitable as these perceptions become inferences about the intrinsic worth or importance of individual programs. The only saving grace is that such debate, difficult and emotional though it may become, is likely to be no more heated or divisive than the uproar that is almost certain to ensue from selective cuts based on some unknown administrative rationale.

Many researchers warn that it is especially difficult to develop and obtain consensus on institutional mission statements during times of scarcity (Dooris and Lozier, 1990; Zammuto, 1986). The true nature of the college or university as a competing collection of special interests becomes most evident at such times (Sibley, 1986). For the same reasons, the development of a vision statement and the articulation of its implications are far easier to accomplish when the college or university is not facing imminent fiscal pressures. However, if financial pressures become sufficiently severe, the institution may have no choice but to belatedly chart its future in order to rationalize a budget-cutting strategy. Difficult and stressful as this leadership challenge may be, it has its rewards: recognition by the campus community that decisions made under conditions of scarcity are driven by a commitment to reaching a shared vision (Parker, 1986) and implicit acceptance by the campus community of budgetary cutbacks that may be locally augmented or exaggerated to permit positive progress toward the vision, even as some campus units are subjected to drastic cutback (Volkwein, 1984).

Selecting the Appropriate Strategy

For most colleges and universities, even a detailed vision statement is unlikely to reveal an unambiguous path for improvement. In general, an institution's response to scarcity must take into account a complex system of overlapping instructional, research, and service programs. What is required, therefore, is some means of systematically sorting these programs and identifying the ones that will best facilitate progress toward the vision. This identification is accomplished through the development of specific criteria by which existing programs and alternative strategies can be analyzed and priorities can be assigned.

Identifying Criteria. Institutional research offices can be particularly useful in helping their institutions to develop evaluative criteria. The types of criteria and guidelines commonly used in assessing and developing priorities for college and university programs include the following (Belanger and Tremblay, 1982; Dube and Brown, 1983; Shirley and Volkwein, 1978): centrality of the program or activity to the institution's mission; existing or potential quality of the program or its "products"; program costs, including implicit or indirect institutional support costs; demand on the part of prospective students and future employers; and pertinent political considerations and other externally driven factors.

Evaluative studies are not only difficult to carry out, they can sometimes be misleading or unexpectedly controversial. For example, except for programs clearly on the periphery of the curriculum, it is not easy to determine how central individual academic programs or service activities are to an abstractly stated institutional mission. For this reason, a vision statement articulated in terms of future institutional characteristics can make it easier to assess how individual programs or activities might contribute to the desired institutional future.

Similarly, quality in the academic area has always been difficult to assess. Judgments based on the quality of academic inputs (number and reputation of faculty, physical facilities, budget and other resources) are far easier to develop than judgments based on outputs (effectiveness of instruction, quality of graduates, importance of research), although the shortcomings of this approach are obvious. To the extent to which the vision statement specifies the outputs of the institution's future characteristics, the analysis of quality can more easily be based on output criteria pertinent to the institution's mission.

Analysis of political considerations can take place more fully and explicitly in executive suites than in institutional research offices. Nevertheless, such factors as uniqueness of the program within the state or region, special sources of current or potential financial support, and strength of alumni or other special-interest group advocacy constitute special criteria that often increase in importance with the magnitude of the scarcity. Even if institutional research staff are not fully privy to such sensitive assessments, they should be prepared to conduct needed background investigation. Again, the institution's capacity for effective environmental scanning will help to determine the confidence with which external considerations can be incorporated into subsequent decision making.

Selecting Criteria. One of the key challenges for institutional research staff is to lead the institution in identifying the criteria that are most pertinent to the decisions that the institution must make. The appropriate choice of criteria can be expected to vary with the magnitude, duration, and political context of the scarcity. The proper choice of evaluative criteria is critical, for it drives the remainder of the decision-making process. For decisions to be implemented successfully, the campus community must not only accept the criteria but acknowledge that programs and activities scoring low on the criteria will be the most vulnerable to possible cutbacks.

Such support can be expected from the campus only when the evaluative criteria are highly credible and broadly understood. Toward this end, identification and elaboration of the criteria call for a highly structured, participative process involving all major campus constituencies (Hyatt, Schulman, and Santiago, 1984; Mortimer and Taylor, 1984). The responsibility of the institutional research office in this phase of the process is not so much one of developing the criteria as it is of helping to design the participative process and then ensuring its integrity.

As with development of mission and vision statements, the proactive institution will begin to identify evaluative criteria long before the full impact of scarcity is experienced. Not only does this allow time for deliberate discussion and full consultation, it permits criteria to be developed in a relatively rational, emotionally neutral atmosphere, one that minimizes argumentation based on self-interest and turf protection (Bloomfield, 1988).

The institutional research office can and should play a significant role in this process: first in helping to design the participative process, then in monitoring the integrity of the analysis and usefulness of the results. Schmidtlein and Milton (1990) emphasize the findings of others that institutional research staff should facilitate the planning, evaluation, and decision making. But they should not expect to be the planners, evaluators, or decision makers, especially in the emotionally charged atmosphere of budget reductions. Their key responsibility is to ensure that evaluative criteria are developed and defined in ways that will allow programs and activities to be measured. As campus leadership orchestrates the identification of criteria, institutional research staff must work to assure that they are defined so as to be measurable and valid (Borden and Delaney, 1989).

What Should Be Measured?

Historically, one primary responsibility of the institutional research office has been to measure and evaluate campus programs and activities. While the quantitative studies traditionally carried out to support allocation decisions remain valid and useful for decision making under scarcity, the analysis tends to be more closely read and the need for careful, complete investigation becomes more critical as conditions deteriorate and the stakes increase. Traditional institutional research analyses commonly focus on enrollment trends, resource utilization, cost allocation, outcomes assessment, demand forecasts, and peer comparisons.

Enrollment trend studies track the number of students majoring in various disciplines and the student credit hours generated in various course sequences. Front-end studies focus on changes in numbers of applications and yield rates. Back-end studies analyze graduation rates and years to completion.

Resource utilization studies track measures of efficiency or productivity (such as student-teacher ratios or administrative expense ratios) in the application of institutional resources. However, productivity ratios can be misleading for service organizations unless they are joined with indicators of quality. For example, do high expense ratios for student advising indicate that advising is inefficient or that students are receiving an enviable level of service?

Cost allocation studies track expenditures by academic or administrative unit or by programmatic activity. They can be done on the basis of direct cost, or they can be full-costing studies that incorporate a prorated allocation of indirect institutional costs.

Outcomes assessment tracks the success of students graduating from the institution's academic programs or measures the benefits accruing from the institution's research or service activities. In contrast to most other analytical studies, outcomes assessment usually requires survey research extending to the institution's external publics.

Demand forecasts predict future demand for higher education services. They can be cohort studies dependent on demographic analyses, or they can take the form of work force demand analyses based on governmental reports and the institution's own environmental scanning.

Peer comparisons gather data from comparable institutions to add perspective to the other types of analysis just reviewed. The credibility of such studies depends on the institutions selected for comparison and on the ability of those institutions to supply the data requested in a truly comparable format.

Ironically, even as these kinds of quantitative analysis become more crucial to informed decision making under scarcity, they may become less definitive as data are skewed by scarcity. Enrollment studies can be biased by shifts in behaviors reflecting efforts by students and prospective students to second-guess future departmental reductions or eliminations. Cost studies can be skewed by shifts in departmental expenditure patterns as institutional units stockpile equipment and supplies or resort to unorthodox personnel management tactics in preparation for possible cutbacks. Peer comparisons can become misleading as comparative institutions undergo severe financial cutbacks: Some comparative institutions may become too preoccupied to provide accurate or adequate data, or peer data may be biased by idiosyncratic campus priorities reflecting the peer institutions' own scarcity-driven resource reallocations.

It is most important—especially when time and staffing are at a premium—for analysis to be consistent with the types of decisions being contemplated and with the decision-making process that the institution follows. Anecdotal evidence suggests that the type of information and analysis most pertinent to a decision tends to change as scarcity rises from easily manageable to crisis proportions, meaning that budget cuts ranging between 2 and

20 percent a year are required. Some types of analysis (such as enrollment trends or program demand) that are extremely useful when moderately scarce resources must be reallocated are much less relevant when programs are targeted in an effort to sharpen or redefine the institution's mission. In contrast, peer comparisons can become more important when the college or university seeks evidence that large-scale efficiencies can be obtained, for example, by restructuring administrative processes.

Finally, a new type of analysis starts assuming value as the scarcity reaches crisis proportions: It suddenly becomes exceedingly important for central administration to know exactly how various activities are conducted throughout the institution. Particularly in large colleges or universities, responsibility for critical activities is commonly decentralized to academic units or relatively independent administrative offices. Faced with potential disastrous scarcity and the likelihood that campus units will have to be eliminated, the institution's top leadership needs confirmation that existing campus processes are already operating as efficiently as possible. As I note later, the conceptual framework of the total quality movement and the analytical tools of process improvement can become a new and useful focus for institutional research studies.

How Will Students React?

As conditions of scarcity become more severe, decision makers must increasingly consider significant sources of new revenues or new strategies for drastically reducing expenditures. In either case, institutional research staff should be prepared to factor into their analyses the estimated impacts of such changes on the institution's key clientele: the students.

The most obvious source of significant revenue enhancement is increased tuition. The question that must be addressed is the degree to which tuition increases will affect future student enrollment. A number of authors have investigated the price elasticity of student demand. They have focused primarily on the enrollment decisions of first-time students; St. John (1990) provides an extensive bibliography and expands this analysis to include the effect of price elasticity on the continuing enrollment decisions of current students. However, these studies can be no more than suggestive for price elasticity analysis at other institutions. Although studies are commonly adjusted for such student variables as socioeconomic status, previous education, and student aspirations, the local circumstances characteristic of the institution or its competitive environment may be overriding determinants of enrollment or persistence decisions. Such local circumstances include the voluntary mobility of the institution's students, the availability of similar academic programs at nearby colleges, and the strength of the local economy and job market.

Similar analytical problems occur in assessing the likely effects of expenditure reductions. A common strategy for expenditure reduction under even moderate conditions of scarcity is the downsizing or elimination of selected academic programs. Cost savings in such downsizing come principally from the termination of faculty and staff associated with the targeted programs. Such a cost reduction strategy often leaves unstated its presumptions about the behavior of students presently enrolled in these programs. If all students choose to remain at the institution, there would be no negative impact on revenues, but it is likely that staffing would have to increase in some other disciplines to accommodate the transferring students. If all students choose to leave the institution to pursue their chosen major elsewhere, the targeted cost reduction would be largely realized (minus legal fees) but at the expense of a countervailing loss in tuition revenues. The actual situation, of course, will be somewhere between these two extremes.

The behavior of current and prospective students in reaction to a decrease in academic programs might be termed the *program elasticity* of student demand. Global studies of program elasticity might be of some assistance, but again the actual effects are likely to be dominated by the institution's local context and conditions. Absent proven theories of price and program elasticity, the institutional research office can provide a valuable service by ensuring that scarcity-driven decision making considers these phenomena.

Financial analysis of proposed cutback strategies may significantly understate or overstate the actual outcome if erroneous assumptions are made about student behavior. Given our incomplete understanding of these two types of elasticity, the most defensible analytical strategy is to develop alternative scenarios based on plausible student behaviors and to base the ultimate decision on explicit consideration of the range of results that could occur. Institutional research offices must be prepared to assist college and university management by providing such decision-driven policy analyses.

What About the Administration?

Faculty beliefs to the contrary, administrative activities—particularly those carried out in separately constituted administrative service units—are not immune to serious scrutiny in scarcity-driven budget reductions (Wergin and Braskamp, 1987). Here, too, the institution seeks to identify activities that are less successful or less central to the institution's fundamental purposes. As in the academic arena, such a strategy has limited uses. It is easy to identify the peripheral and ailing activities. Once they have been eliminated, how do we identify activities suitable for reduction or elimination in the next round of cuts?

The concepts of total quality now being embraced by the business world suggest a new strategy for dealing with the impact of scarcity on administrative activities. One basic tenet of the quality movement is that an organization operates through a succession of processes and that the organization improves only if these individual processes improve. The administration of a college or university operates through organizational units responsible for a large number of interrelated processes. It is the totality of these processes, not the organizational framework in which they operate, that makes the institution's administration more or less effective and more or less costly. Viewed from the perspective of total quality, scarcity-driven cost reduction should focus not so much on the elimination of administrative units and activities but rather on the redesign and reorganization of the administrative activities that must continue. The analytical tools of process improvement enable a college or university to understand how its resources are being marshalled in the performance of administrative processes and to see how a restructuring and redistribution of these processes could reduce costs without decreasing functionality.

This is not to say that there are not administrative processes that we could reasonably leave undone or reduce in scope. As colleges and universities have continued to grow and as administrators have tried to provide the wide range of services requested by the campus community and the public, new administrative functions and organizational units have proliferated. The movement throughout higher education to integrate campus services vertically has only added to this growing administrative apparatus. The result is an increasing number of institutional functions that at best are only peripherally related to the institution's principal mission.

Finally, impatience with the response from centralized administrative services has often led academic departments and other operating units to duplicate such activities as financial record keeping, research coordination, personnel management, and student placement locally. While such local shadow systems have resulted in arguably better service to the department's faculty and students, they can tie up institutional resources out of proportion to their incremental effectiveness. Where duplication of effort is rampant, the consolidation of processes can yield substantial savings without eliminating any administrative services.

A study of administrative processes undertaken at Oregon State University established criteria by which efficient administrative processes can be identified (KPMG Peat Marwick, 1992). Such processes have found ways to do things once and do them right. They have reengineered procedures to reduce the staff time required. Unnecessary steps, levels of review, and signatures required have been eliminated. Processes have been centralized where appropriate to achieve economies of scale. Duplicate, parallel structures and processes have been eliminated. Decision making and responsibility have been pushed to the lowest possible staff level. The environment is one of trust; decisions are not continually verified. Finally, these processes have improved customer satisfaction.

Through scientific, data-based analysis of their critical processes, commercial and industrial enterprises have improved the effectiveness of their operations and their bottom-line results. Colleges and universities that have applied these concepts to their administrative activities have seen similar positive results (Coate, 1992). Rather than seeking activities to eliminate, these institutions are using process improvement techniques to restructure and reorganize administrative processes to the institution's benefit. While the tools of quality improvement were not designed as cost-cutting methods, they can help colleges and universities to identify new ways of responding to conditions of scarcity. These quality tools, by their very nature, depend heavily on the type of expertise found in institutional research offices. By developing staff expertise in process improvement and quality enhancement methodologies, an institutional research office can reinforce its image as a valuable campus resource.

Conclusion

As conditions of scarcity range from easily manageable to near catastrophic, the conceptual framework and analytical tools used for decision making will vary. For any level of financial hardship, the colleges and universities that are best prepared to face the challenge will be those that have established effective mechanisms well before the hardship occurs. Such mechanisms will include a systematic program of environmental scanning, mission and vision statements with clearly articulated implications for the institution, and a process for identifying the criteria to be used in evaluating institutional programs and establishing priorities among them.

Each of these prerequisites for success in addressing scarcity-driven decisions should be both vigorously promoted and analytically guided by the institutional research office. Recognizing that any of these activities is difficult to start (let alone bring to consensus) once the institution is suffering from scarcity, institutional research staff need to be persistent in arguing that they should be undertaken well before their results are needed.

The second arena in which offices of institutional research should assume an advocacy role is in the adoption of a quality ethic and a process improvement methodology for the analysis of institutional activities. Even when scarcity is not a motivating factor, colleges and universities should feel obligated to demonstrate a commitment to effectiveness, efficiency, and quality in all their undertakings. As the external public and internal campus constituencies become more aware and appreciative of quality-conscious business and service organizations, they will increasingly expect colleges and universities to adopt a similar approach to their academic and administrative services.

References

Belanger, C. H., and Tremblay, L. "A Methodological Approach to Selective Cutbacks." *Canadian Journal of Higher Education*, 1982, 12 (3), 25–35.

Bloomfield, S. D. "Both Sides Now: Yet Another Look at Resource Reallocation." Paper presented to the Academy on Budget, Resource Planning, and Development at the annual meeting of the Society for College and University Planning, 1988.

Borden, M. H., and Delaney, E. L. "Information Support for Group Decision Making." In P. T. Ewell (ed.), *Enhancing Information Use in Decision Making*. New Directions for Institutional Research, no. 64. San Francisco: Jossey-Bass, 1989.

Bowen, F. M., and Glenny, L. A. *Uncertainty in Public Higher Education: Responses to Stress at Ten California Colleges and Universities*. Sacramento: California Postsecondary Education Commission, 1980.

Chaffee, E. E. "Successful Strategic Management in Small Private Colleges." *Journal of Higher Education*, 1984, 55 (2), 212–241.

Coate, L. E. *Total Quality Management at Oregon State University*. Corvallis: Office of the President, Oregon State University, 1992.

Davies, G. K. "The Importance of Being General: Philosophy, Politics, and Institutional Mission Statements." In J. Smart (ed.), *Higher Education: Handbook of Theory and Research*. Vol. 2. New York: Agathon Press, 1986.

Dooris, N. J., and Lozier, G. G. "Adopting Formal Planning Approaches: The Pennsylvania State University." In F. A. Schmidtlein and T. H. Milton (eds.), *Adapting Strategic Planning to Campus Realities*. New Directions for Institutional Research, no. 67. San Francisco: Jossey-Bass, 1990.

Dube, C. W., and Brown, A. W. "Strategic Assessment: A Rational Response to University Cutbacks." *Long-Range Planning*, 1983, 16, 105–113.

Hyatt, J. A., Schulman, C. H., and Santiago, A. A. *Reallocation Strategies for Effective Resource Management*. Washington, D.C.: National Association of College and University Business Officers, 1984.

Keller, G. A. *Academic Strategy: The Management Revolution in American Higher Education*. Baltimore, Md.: Johns Hopkins University Press, 1983.

KPMG Peat Marwick. *Administrative Cost/Structure Assessment of Oregon State University*. New York: KPMG Peat Marwick, 1992.

Lang, D. W., and Lopers-Sweetman, R. "The Role of Statements of Institutional Purpose." *Research in Higher Education*, 1991, 32 (6), 599–624.

Mortimer, K. P., and Taylor, B. E. "Budgeting Strategies Under Conditions of Decline." In L. L. Leslie (ed.), *Responding to New Realities in Funding*. New Directions for Institutional Research, no. 43. San Francisco: Jossey-Bass, 1984.

Oregon State University. *Oregon State University: Beginning the Twenty-First Century*. Corvallis: Office of the President, Oregon State University, 1992.

Parker, B. "Agreement of Mission and Institutional Responses to Decline." *Research in Higher Education*, 1986, 25 (2), 164–181.

St. John, E. P. "Price Response in Persistence Decisions: An Analysis of the High School and Beyond Senior Cohort." *Research in Higher Education*, 1990, 31 (4), 387–403.

Schmidtlein, F. A., and Milton, T. H. (eds.). *Adapting Strategic Planning to Campus Realities*. New Directions for Institutional Research, no. 67. San Francisco: Jossey-Bass, 1990.

Shirley, R. C., and Volkwein, J. F. "Establishing Academic Program Priorities." *Journal of Higher Education*, 1978, 49, 472–488.

Sibley, W. M. "Strategic Planning and Management for Change." *Canadian Journal of Higher Education*, 1986, 16 (2), 81–101.

Volkwein, J. F. "Responding to Financial Retrenchment: Lessons from the Albany Experience." *Journal of Higher Education*, 1984, 55, 398–401.

Wergin, J. F., and Braskamp, L. A. (eds.). *Evaluating Administrative Services and Programs*. New Directions for Institutional Research, no. 56. San Francisco: Jossey-Bass, 1987.

Zammuto, R. F. "Managing Decline in American Higher Education." In J. Smart (ed.), *Higher Education: Handbook of Theory and Research*. Vol. 2. New York: Agathon Press, 1986.

STEFAN D. BLOOMFIELD is professor of finance and international business in the College of Business at Oregon State University, Corvallis, and was senior assistant to the university president for five years.

Decisions about scarce resources affect people most of all. This chapter discusses who should make these decisions and how they should be made.

Participants in Decisions About Scarce Resources

Judith M. Gappa

Colleges and universities have moved into an era of scarce and diminishing resources. Lazerson and Wagener (1992, p. 44) paint a grim picture of the current fiscal situation: "Harvard University's deficit last year was $42 million; Columbia University is projecting a $50 million loss for 1992–1993. Yale University's announced plans to cut 11 percent of its faculty have engendered heated controversy. And across the nation, institutions' costs for medical benefits, deferred maintenance, and financial aid are spiraling upward; no one can even predict the educational and fiscal impact of abolishing a mandatory age for faculty retirement."

Despite the growing financial woes of higher education, the American people view it with ambivalence rather than sympathy. While it is seen as essential to improving national competitiveness, creating new knowledge, and providing equal opportunity, higher education is also seen as costly and wasteful. Its leaders are perceived as making excuses for failure to progress on important national goals while complaining about inadequate funding, even when resources are stable or growing (Massy, 1992). In short, colleges and universities will have to change drastically in the face of declining dollars and a somewhat hostile national environment.

To meet the challenges of the 1990s and beyond will require effective decision making and a high degree of teamwork. Colleges and universities differ from other organizations in the emphasis that their constituencies place on participation in internal decision-making processes, including those that involve the allocation of scarce resources. The importance of constituent participation was illustrated by events at San Diego State University during the

NEW DIRECTIONS FOR INSTITUTIONAL RESEARCH, no. 79, Fall 1993   © Jossey-Bass Publishers

summer of 1992. After the president proposed laying off 146 tenured and tenure-track faculty in the face of budget cuts, 59 percent of the academic senate voted no confidence in him, 56 percent of the faculty asked the California State University (CSU) System to replace him, and the faculty union invited the American Association of University Professors to examine his actions. Students staged a twenty-four-hour vigil to protest state budget cuts and his actions. While the CSU chancellor supported the president, he also said, "What makes it unhealthy is not what you do but how you do it in an academic institution. Those that will prosper from this activity [budget cutting] will do it more because the way they went through it was healthy than because the solutions they reached were marvelously ingenious" (Lively, 1992, p. A21).

This chapter seeks to help institutions establish healthy decision processes appropriate to their individual circumstances and needs. It explores two main issues: who should make decisions about managing with scarce resources and how these decisions should be made. Three models are examined.

Underlying these models are two fundamental principles. First, faculty are the heart of the institution. Faculty are not simply employees of a college or university. They are, instead, persons whose expertise, training, and function within their institution render their judgment indispensable when decisions that affect academic policies and programs are made. Second, successful colleges and universities are governed through the active, informed participation of all constituents. According to Wolvin (1991), the tradition of shared governance in most institutions of higher education includes all constituents with each participating according to its functions and responsibilities. While the faculty has the fundamental role and primary responsibility for the academic mission, staff and students also have responsibility for participation in academic, administrative, and quality-of-life issues that affect them. At the bottom line, participation by all stakeholders makes decisions more healthy and more likely to be accepted.

Choosing a Decision-Making Model

The particular decision-making model or style that an institution adopts is based primarily on its mission, size, complexity, and culture. Each college or university must decide for itself—based on its traditions, leadership, and current situation—how decisions regarding scarce resources are going to be made. To the extent possible, well-established institutional decision-making processes should be used.

Each institution's resource allocation decisions are constantly being shaped by external forces, such as demographic shifts, economic growth or decline, new governmental initiatives, or new laws or systemwide policies. They are also shaped by the values and aspirations of each institution's leaders, typically the president, members of the governing board, the chief academic officer, and faculty members. These leaders, especially new ones, may articulate a different role for the institution. But the most powerful factor in shaping a college or university's decisions is its culture. An institution's culture evolves over time based on patterns of routine interactions among students, faculty, institutional leaders, and alumni. It can help or hinder the institution's ability to deal effectively with a rapidly changing external environment.

In most colleges and universities, faculty members—the primary carriers of institutional culture—assume responsibility for establishing and modifying academic programs and policies. Increasingly, then, faculty must be willing to involve themselves in the difficult choices that scarce and declining resources require. The selection and socialization of new faculty are critical in maintaining well-established, effective decision-making processes for this purpose. The projected turnover in faculty (340,000 new faculty appointments by the year 2005) presents a major challenge (Chronister, 1991). As large cohorts of senior faculty retire, a major source of institutional memory may be lost just as new faculty are learning the values and culture of their institution. At a time when colleges and universities are experiencing an external mandate to do more with less, their most precious resource for decision making, the faculty, may be least well prepared to make the critical choices that the reality of scarce resources requires.

Shared Governance Model

Shared governance and participatory decision making are well-established traditions at most colleges and universities.

The philosophical underpinnings of shared governance are codified in the American Association of University Professors (AAUP) (1990) *Policy Documents and Reports.* a publication commonly referred to as the "Redbook." The basic tenet of shared governance is that the management of academic institutions requires a joint effort. "The variety and complexity of tasks performed by institutions of higher education produce an inescapable interdependence among governing board, administration, faculty, students, and others. The relationship calls for adequate communication among these components and full opportunity for appropriate joint planning and effort" (AAUP, 1990, p. 120).

This joint effort or shared governance is essential in budgeting and resource allocation decision making. "The allocation of resources among competing demands is central in the formal responsibility of the governing board, in the administrative authority of the president, and in the educational function of the faculty. Each component should, therefore, have a voice in the determination of short- and long-range priorities, and each should receive appropriate analyses of past budgetary experience, reports on current budgets and expenditures, and short- and long-range budgetary projections. The function of each component in budgetary matters should be understood by all; the allocation of authority will determine the flow of information and the scope of participation in decisions" (AAUP, 1990, p. 121). According to AAUP, the scope of the faculty role should include preparation of the total institutional budget, decisions about allocations to specific fiscal divisions, and policies and procedures governing salary increases. In conditions of fiscal exigency, the faculty should be informed as early and as specifically as possible and should participate at the department, school, and institution levels in decision making about the future of the institution and specific academic programs.

In the 1980s, AAUP embraced collective bargaining. "As a national organization which has historically played a major role in formulating and implementing the principles that govern relationships in academic life, the Association promotes collective bargaining to reinforce the best features of higher education. The principles of academic freedom and tenure, fair procedures, faculty participation in governance, and the primary responsibility of the faculty for determining academic policy will thereby be secured" (AAUP, 1990, p. 145). AAUP does not see collective bargaining as making substantive changes in shared governance. Quite the contrary, AAUP views collective bargaining as strengthening shared governance by specifying and ensuring the faculty role in institutional decision making. Gilmour (1991, p. 16) showed that 60 percent of collective bargaining agreements recognize a separate faculty governance body and that the relationship between the collective bargaining unit and the governance body is viewed as complementary or actively supportive 78 percent of the time.

History shows that so-called dual-track governance, in which the faculty union negotiates on behalf of shared governance, considerably strengthens the role of faculty senates in decision making. In California, for example, the Higher Education Employee Relations Act (HEERA)—the enabling legislation for collective bargaining—provides for and defines the responsibilities of both the academic senate and the exclusive representative. In the California State University system, many individuals actively participate in both. "I, in fact, served on the bargaining team at the same time that I served as local senate chair . . . by virtue of my office as senate chair, I also sit with my campus president's executive staff. Some of us wondered . . . if my union responsibilities might not conflict with my senate responsibilities in the latter capacity. Such conflicts have, however, simply not arisen, and these different roles have proven complementary in nature" (Schaefer, 1987, p. 12). Many in higher education would disagree with this assessment. They would assert instead that dual-track governance has made relationships with the administration increasingly adversarial and in some cases diminished the effectiveness of traditional governance bodies.

Despite some conflicts inherent in collective bargaining, the preeminent role of the faculty in making decisions that affect academic programs and the concept of shared governance pervade higher education and dominate decision structures in most colleges and universities. In a study of responses from faculty and administrators at 402 institutions, Gilmour (1991, p. 16) found that 91 percent of the respondents had a faculty governing body. Seventy-nine percent of the respondents agreed or strongly agreed with positive statements about the composition, effectiveness, and issue orientation of their governing bodies—a finding that clearly counters the general perception that faculty senates are beleaguered from without and stultified within. However, the unwieldy nature of senates and the slowness of the deliberative process impede their effectiveness when current situations demand rapid responses to external conditions.

Corporate Management Model

Increased competition for students, stable or declining resources, and public demands for accountability have led some institutions of higher education to adopt features of corporate managerial structures. The perceived and actual transfer of power from faculty to the administration and boards of trustees is driven in part by frustration with the difficulty that traditional faculty governance structures have in reaching consensus and in taking decisive and timely action. Some believe that faculty lack the will and expertise necessary to make the hard decisions required for survival in an era of scarce resources.

While faculty fear that an ever-expanding and increasingly specialized administration is usurping their voice in decision making, administrators contend that faculty are less willing to be engaged in university life unless it affects their narrow interests. Faculty no longer dwell in splendid isolation on their campuses. As they become more cosmopolitan and diverse, their loyalties become complex. Junior faculty, immersed in a struggle for tenure, find university service rarely rewarded. All faculty are members of their discipline, to which many give their primary allegiance. The predominance of the discipline and rapid advances in technology allow many faculty to do their work while spending little or no time at their institution. As faculty have become less involved in campus decision making, administrators with training in business or educational administration and law are filling the void. Faculty reactions to the increase in administration are often negative. According to Levinson (1989, pp. 23–24), "The faculty . . . perspective may be less appreciated by the MBAs on their way to cost-effective and rapid decisions. Their norms may not recognize the value of muddling through the design or rationale of an academic program in the quest for a balanced curriculum. 'Efficiency' may require that faculty only react to decisions rather than participate in making them. Similarly, attorneys serving in roles of university counsel or in other administrative positions may allow the 'courtroom culture' to overwhelm a community of trust."

While some faculty may decry what is happening, the rise of a corporate culture and the use of management tools have helped colleges and universities survive in an increasingly competitive world. Sophistication in the management of resources is essential as colleges and universities are transformed from communal societies to corporate entities.

> College and university budgets range from $500,000 to over $1 billion per year; the magnitude of financial responsibility dictates many institutional management requirements and processes. Many colleges and universities are in the category of "big business" and therefore require the same kind of expert management that is found in business and industry. . . . The management of a college or university is made even more complex by the lack of a traditional bottom line. . . . There is no simple, widely accepted measure of success or failure for either the total organization or for many of its parts in the way that "profit" represents success in commercial organizations [Ford, 1992, p. 5].

And yet, no matter how essential the incorporation of some features of corporate management may be, chief business officers continue to believe that faculty have a crucial role in decisions about resource allocation. "In every higher education institution, no matter what its size, there are never enough resources for everything that the deans, department heads, faculty, and students would like to have done. Therefore, it is necessary . . . to develop priorities . . . Input should be gathered from deans, department heads, faculty, and students before these priorities are set" (Ford, 1992, p. 12).

Keller (1983) foresaw the move toward incorporating features of corporate management into higher education a decade ago. In his controversial book *Academic Strategy: The Management Revolution in American Higher Education,* he asserted that colleges and universities lacked adequate planning, strong internal management, and a clear set of academic objectives. A quote from Clark Kerr captured his view of the situation: "Full autonomy—to the extent it ever existed—is dead. The greatest change in governance now going on is not the rise of student power or faculty power but the rise of public power" (Keller, 1983, pp. 24–25).

Who, then, will lead the management revolution that Keller thinks higher education so desperately needs? He suggests that administrators will replace faculty who "have no stomach for leading the way during contraction and little desire for selecting academic priorities among their own efforts" (Keller, 1983, p. 59). In his now famous (or infamous) statement, Keller (1983, p. 61) described governance as "the old, looping Ping-Pong game between the administration and the faculty" and declared it was no longer adequate since "academic senates are slowly collapsing or becoming dormant." He proposed that a Joint Big Decisions Committee, made up of administrators, faculty, and students, be instituted for the purpose of providing the president with advice and guidance on what to do, and that its deliberations be secret. In sum, Keller tried to bring together management concepts and shared governance traditions to achieve an ideal solution to higher education's problems. In his view, the ideal solution is for faculty to concede executive power and authority for overall planning and priority setting to academic management in exchange for the opportunity to examine these plans and priorities with the "full strength of their critical and analytical expertise" (Keller, 1983, p. 62).

It is predictable that faculty steeped in the philosophy of shared governance have shown little enthusiasm for these ideas. For example, Bilik and Blum (1989, p. 10) characterized the new corporate management style as "a hierarchical pyramid of control with one ultimate source of final authority; nurturing of strong dependency relationships on superiors; top-down decision-making and communication; centralized planning and coordination; and authoritarian and admittedly intrusive management."

Total Quality Management Model

Seymour (1992, p. 5) highlights the public's "dwindling confidence in [the] ability [of higher education] to provide quality services at a reasonable cost." Espousing the belief that Total Quality Management (TQM) can and should be applied to higher education, Seymour suggests that "if improved quality is the goal, then the way to achieve it is to ask the people who work *in the system* to join with management to work *on the system*" (p. 17). But TQM's endorsement of participation has very little, if any, resemblance to traditional academic governance structures. Participation in TQM means teamwork to achieve quality improvements at all levels within the organization.

The basic premise of TQM is continuous improvement in the quality of the services and products that the organization provides to customers. This improvement is accomplished by focusing on the processes that make up the system. Improvements in the system and its products are made by people who work together on a day-by-day basis in cross-functional teams. These teams analyze existing processes and suggest new ways of simplifying systems and preventing problems. "Teams are at the heart of TQM. Better solutions emerge when everyone involved has a chance to work on process problems. Equally important, solutions are implemented faster and last longer because the people affected have helped to develop them" (Coate, 1991, p. 34).

As resources tighten in higher education, some colleges and universities have been motivated to adopt TQM principles. However, acceptance of the idea that students, alumni, and the public are customers and that working in cross-functional teams can improve services to customers can be difficult, particularly among faculty. As one administrator described it, "I had to sell the vision [of TQM] to the faculty. I had to bring them in, and I have a unionized faculty—a very powerful AFT union. . . . The senate was controlled by the union. What I did was to pull out some of the best union people who are really talented . . . and bring them into the process. We worked and worked, and we destroyed the whole adversarial relationship myth. We replaced it with essentially a trusting, cooperative relationship, and each year they became more deeply involved" (Seymour, 1992, p. 157).

Oregon State University (OSU) has implemented TQM throughout its organization in nine phases. In the early phases, OSU used a planning process to define its mission, understand its customers, identify the functions essential to accomplishing its mission, and state its vision of the future. Then, management teams of no more than ten people who normally work together on the process being reviewed, and who control the resources necessary to improve the processes, were put together. Using a ten-step problem-solving process, these teams began focusing on the customer and on the root causes of and barriers to improvement. The first study teams were in the division of finance and administration. The movement then spread to international education, continuing education, housing, and development. By 1991, twenty teams were operating. Coate (1991) projects that ultimately all employees will be on at least one of four hundred TQM teams, because Oregon State's vision statement identifies TQM as vital not only for the realization of its vision but also for its continued survival in the marketplace.

The TQM philosophy is not without critics. For example, some object to taking consumer (that is, student) satisfaction as a principal guide. These critics charge that TQM is inattentive to core values in the search for efficiency (Pedersen, 1992). But the emphasis that TQM places on involving people in a common quest for quality appears to be consistent with the best features of the shared governance and corporate management approaches in higher education: shared responsibility for decision making and processes aimed at finding and acting on problems promptly and effectively.

Managing in an Era of Constraints and Change

Managing with scarce and diminishing resources can be viewed as a crisis or as an opportunity. Hard times can also be times for making difficult resource choices that can improve the quality of a college or university. In a highly competitive and rapidly changing external environment, every institution must find its own way of becoming more productive and improving its quality while containing costs. This concluding section makes suggestions for achieving that goal.

Colleges and universities are governed best through the active, informed participation of their constituents. When those who are affected by decisions—faculty, staff, students, and external constituents—are involved, better decisions are made, and these decisions are more readily accepted.

The tradition of shared governance is inherent in the role of the faculty.

Administrators manage, staff serve, students come and go, but faculty, by virtue of their professional characteristics and roles, build and maintain the academic policies and programs that define the college or university. Faculty must accept their fundamental responsibility for making tough decisions about the future of the college or university in concert with the administration. Shared governance does not mean that faculty should react to administrative proposals as Keller (1983) has suggested. It means that faculty should join with the administration in anticipating problems or opportunities and help to find solutions.

Each college or university is unique. The structures and processes for shared governance and active participation are the products of distinct cultures, traditions, and current situations. There is no "one size fits all" for approaches to institutional decision making about scarce resources.

Everyone within each academic community is responsible for establishing and maintaining an environment conducive to free discussion. Failure to exercise leadership, the behavioral excesses of groups in pursuit of their own agendas, and failure to adhere to well-established principles for consultation can impair productive relationships and collaborative decision making. Cooperation rather than confrontation can best be achieved by careful attention to the importance of process and the human consequences that result from decision making. Decisions will be better accepted if faculty, staff, and students view them as consultative, fair, and in the institution's best interests.

When possible, difficult choices about scarce and diminishing resources should be made with decision structures that are already in place. Early anticipation of problems and common understandings about who makes what types of decisions and how they will be made are critical. There are many actors on the decision stage. Academic departments build their budget requests for transmittal to deans and then to academic vice presidents. Unions represent the concerns of their members within the scope of bargaining—for example, salary increases, benefits packages, and work load. Campuswide faculty governance groups are concerned about the implications for educational policy, academic programs, and the future of the profession. Other employee, student, and alumni organizations want their voices to be heard. Written policies that define the roles and responsibilities of these various constituencies in decision making about resources are essential for ensuring that confusion about who recommends what to whom and when is kept to a minimum. If established procedures and processes are adhered to in good and bad times, mutual trust is the result.

In order to participate meaningfully, all members of the academic community need accurate, timely, and understandable information. This information should address the current budget and future budgetary constraints. Participants should have time to discuss budgetary matters with their colleagues. Efforts should be made to communicate what is happening so that the entire academic community is kept well informed. In an environment of open and honest communication based on shared knowledge, final decisions about the allocation of scarce resources should contain no surprises.

Meaningful participation must be combined with a sense of urgency. Higher education is driven by competing external forces. In this environment, resource decisions may have to be made much more rapidly, and traditional governance structures may no longer be effective. Shared governance and participation are principles that underlie the academic community; they are not structures. New or reshaped governance structures may become necessary when change occurs rapidly. Institutions must adapt to existing conditions, but they can do so without abandoning their commitment to meaningful participation.

The tradition of shared governance in decisions about resources is well established. Faculty are usually active participants in the development of the operating budget, since it is, in effect, a realization of the institution's academic mission. Faculty should also participate in the development of criteria and methods to be used in situations of financial exigency and retrenchment. However, faculty must accept that there are limits to participation. For example, faculty do not have a right to determine whether financial exigency exists. Nor should faculty governance bodies make decisions about allocations among various departments and activities or about the distribution of salary dollars to individuals. Faculty should do what they do best: collaborate with administrators in establishing the policies, criteria, processes, and procedures for using the resources that are available.

Healthy institutions continuously evaluate the effectiveness of their decision structures and make changes. The alternative is obsolescence and decline: "Of all the troubles that may befall a college or university, perhaps the most unnoticed at the time, yet pervasive and unfortunate, is the drift into pro forma performance. . . . Established ways are adhered to and carried through so as to require the least effort. . . . Partly as cause, partly as effect, administrators with a housekeeping rather than a leadership outlook tend to hold office . . . [and] the various parties reach a mutual accommodation to not disturb the current situation" (Simpson, 1991, p. 201). Pro forma performance is the hallmark of a noncompetitive and declining institution.

In sum, the allocation of scarce resources requires participatory decision structures that address two core issues: Who will be involved in the processes, and how will they be involved? With this understanding and an environment characterized by open communication, respect, and trust, colleges and universities can approach the future confident of their ability to make informed and timely choices in an era of constraints.

References

American Association of University Professors. *Policy Documents and Reports*. Washington, D.C.: American Association of University Professors, 1990.

Bilik, L. J., and Blum, M. C. "Deja Vu All Over Again: Initiatives in Academic Management." *Academe,* 1989, 75 (1), 10–13.

Chronister, J. L. "Institutional Culture and the New Professoriate." *Academe,* 1991, 77 (5), 23–25.

Coate, L. E. "Implementing Total Quality Management in a University Setting." In L. A. Sherr and D. J. Teeter (eds.), *Total Quality Management in Higher Education.* New Directions for Institutional Research, no. 71. San Francisco: Jossey-Bass, 1991.

Ford, F. R. "Business, Financial, and Administrative Functions." In D. M. Greene (ed.), *College and University Business Administration.* Vol. 1. (5th ed.) Washington, D.C.: National Association of College and University Business Officers, 1992.

Gilmour, J. E., Jr. "Your Faculty Senate: More Effective Than You Think?" *Academe,* 1991, 77 (5), 16–19.

Keller, G. *Academic Strategy: The Management Revolution in American Higher Education.* Baltimore, Md.: Johns Hopkins University Press, 1983.

Lazerson, M., and Wagener, U. "Point of View." *Chronicle of Higher Education,* Sept. 30, 1992, p. A44.

Levinson, R. M. "The Faculty and Institutional Isomorphism." *Academe,* 1989, 75 (1), 23–27.

Lively, K. "Deep Cuts in State Spending Produce a Bitter Mood at San Diego State." *Chronicle of Higher Education,* Nov. 4, 1992, p. A21.

Massy, W. F. "Foreword." In D. M. Greene (ed.), *College and University Business Administration.* Vol. 1. (5th ed.) Washington, D.C.: National Association of College and University Business Officers, 1992.

Pedersen, R. F. "The Perils of Total Quality Management: Bringing Business Rhetoric to Academe." *Chronicle of Higher Education,* Sept. 23, 1992, p. B4.

Schaefer, S. D. "The Senate and the Union in the California State University System." *Academe,* 1987, 73 (6), 12–15.

Seymour, D. T. *On Q: Causing Quality in Higher Education.* New York: American Council on Education and Macmillan, 1992.

Simpson, W. B. *Cost Containment for Higher Education: Strategies for Public Policy and Institutional Administration.* New York: Praeger, 1991.

Wolvin, A. D. "When Governance Is Really Shared: The Multi-Constituency Senate." *Academe,* 1991, 77 (5), 26–28.

JUDITH M. GAPPA is vice president for human relations and professor of educational administration at Purdue University, West Lafayette, Indiana, and was associate vice president for faculty affairs at San Francisco State University between 1980 and 1991.

This chapter reviews the issues raised in this volume and identifies the
challenges that lie ahead.

Challenges for the Future

William B. Simpson

In the Editor's Notes of this volume, I distinguished among several interpre-
tations of *resource scarcity* in higher education. In Chapter One, Pickens reviews the principles and steps that an institution can follow in evaluating the
adequacy of its resources. The challenge is to learn from comparisons with
other institutions without becoming a follower. That is, each institution
should seek to perform optimally.

Broadening the Challenge

With survival assured, an institution's goals should be more than to catch up
and maintain an acceptable level of accomplishment. The institution should
seek to improve the selection and quality of its offerings at a rate that antici-
pates the requirements and opportunities of an increasingly complex society.
    Leaders within higher education could take a step in that direction were
they to encourage the development of measures of the adequacy of available
resources relative to full implementation of public policy objectives that have
been adopted for postsecondary education. Such measures are needed for
different functions (instruction, research, outreach, and so forth), for individual institutions, for types of institution, and for state and national aggre-
gates of colleges and universities. The development of such measures calls for
both analytical ability and familiarity with statistical sources, and it should
challenge institutional researchers to contribute their best efforts.
    What should be sought is a better view as to the scale of effort toward
various goals that can be justified in terms of the benefits derived and the resources required. The hope is that such a view will inspire bold efforts to optimize the contribution of higher education. The vision of what higher

New Directions for Institutional Research, no. 79, Fall 1993   © Jossey-Bass Publishers

education can contribute must be communicated to the public, so that citizens appreciate its potential and so that it receives sufficient support.

Primarily Instructional Institutions

The main limitation on increasing tuition and fee revenue is the perceived extent to which the overall benefits created are capturable and can be currently financed. Individuals who do not qualify for financial assistance may be deterred from continuing their education to the socially optimal extent when an institution increases the charges that they must pay in order to finance institution-based programs assisting those who do qualify for financial aid. One strategy for containing total cost through tuition policies is the ex post facto grant approach, which improves access to postsecondary education and reduces cost for both individual institutions and the federal government. Simpson and Mendelson (1986) and Simpson (1987, 1989, 1991) outline this approach. Simpson (1987) includes an extensive bibliography. Collins and Hanson (1992) provide background.

Chapter Two organizes the discussion of options for coping with reduced resources around three themes: defensive reaction, constructive structuring and flexibility, and long-term new directions. One option that Chapter Two does not cover is to admit applicants who require minimal financial assistance while reducing expenditures for programs that motivate and prepare individuals for college and encourage persistence. That option is not reasonable. Motivating individuals to value education and broadening the educational options for minority youth should go forward even when budgets are tight. Chapter Two raised the question of assuring that applicants are adequately prepared to benefit from higher education only to forestall waste of resources that could be predicted.

If enrollment is limited, should all applicants be given an equal opportunity to qualify, or should steps be taken to ensure diversity of enrollment? If diversity is a factor in acceptance, will some youth take admission for granted and prepare less than they would otherwise, and will others regard the policy as reverse discrimination? If diversity is not a factor in acceptance and if equal treatment of applications does not produce diversity, are we sending a discouraging message to youth who should be encouraged? However these questions are answered, the mentoring activities and the individual commitment discussed in Chapter Two are important. Commitment would be encouraged if students accepted the view that I stressed in a recent article (Simpson, 1993): While assistance from others, including the government, can be critical, success ultimately depends on activation of the individual's own inner resources.

Pickens states there is a general consensus that compelling demands on resources will prevent the total amount of federal support for higher education from increasing in real dollars. He quotes advice from the president of

Princeton University for research institutions, which he extends to primarily instructional institutions: Adopt a realistic strategy, and meet world-class standards in all programs that one decides to keep or begin. A more realistic policy would be the selective depth-of-offering approach described in Chapter Two, which combines needed breadth with needed economy of operation.

What I recommend is that every institution identify more clearly than it does now the fundamental objectives that it wants to serve. Then it should restructure its instructional program so as to bear more directly on the accomplishment of those objectives. The mission of higher education can be viewed as including the development in individuals of rational and creative capacity, competence in an area of application, and enhanced appreciation of relationships within an expanded boundary of concern.

Organizing teaching on the basis of academic disciplines serves various curriculum needs, but it may not in all instances produce the best arrangement (Hearn, 1992). One possible basis for restructuring, which an institution could implement in any of several different ways as dictated by its view of its purposes, is what Chapter Two referred to as goal-oriented learning. Goal-oriented learning requires a shift away from the subject-centered teaching that has attracted individuals to the academic profession. While the institution would still offer faculty members an environment conducive to their own intellectual pursuits, it would remove the presumption that the path to further student accomplishment coincides with a faculty member's personal direction of interest. Goal-oriented learning would require faculty incentive systems to emphasize students almost as much as they now do scholarship. Finally, goal-oriented learning could mean that those attracted into teaching and remaining therein would be those whose personal enthusiasm made them, along with their students, comrades in the quest.

Challenge of Technology

Norris emphasizes in Chapter Three that the use of technology in instruction cannot simply be an add-on if it is to help institutions contain costs. Instead, the teaching-learning system must be transformed. Instructional technology can facilitate self-paced, interactive learning that is programmed according to an individual's learning style and learning goals. If it were used in this way, faculty would shift from lecturing to facilitating and mentoring individual learning activity, and students would assume more responsibility than they now do. Collaboration among institutions in preparing computer-based learning resources would make economies of scale possible. The education process would become more decentralized and depend less on the campus as its center.

In reflecting on these possible developments, I see several challenges. First, can institutions avoid spreading faculty members' time too thinly among students? Will the faculty member be forced to become the manager for a team of low-cost learning assistants? Second, postsecondary education is a set of experiences involving access to teachers and library resources, inter-relationships with fellow students and staff, identification with a campus and its heritage, learning from assuming responsibility and working together, and so forth. A student's goals may evolve from any of the experiences just listed, even during a single class period when the teacher is inspired and the student is receptive. Can a student's decentralized interactive relationship with a computer substitute adequately for the above? Third, will learning resources designed in collaboration among institutions address the lowest common denominator? Will it screen out all but prevailing viewpoints and modes of approach? Will the individual nature of course content be unduly influenced by the availability of materials prepared off campus? Fourth, will faculty members be given the time needed to be both informed about and creative with respect to developments in their fields? Fifth, will the cost of attracting and holding faculty increase when the managerial and facilitating skills required of faculty are skills that can be marketed in the business world? If that cost increases and it is not met, what will be the quality of faculty?

For British and Canadian experience, see Percival, Craig, and Buglass (1987) and Snowden and Daniel (1980). Albright and Graf (1992), Hefzallah (1990), Jackson (1990), and Munshi (1980) also address this topic.

MacDonald also stresses, in Chapter Three, the need for decentralized systems and more sophisticated campus data networks (see also Emery, 1980). Three issues concern me in this context. First, arguments for increased use of technology in administration tend to emphasize increased efficiency. That is, the ratio of benefit to cost goes up. They neglect to note that this can reflect total benefit increasing without there necessarily being a decrease in total cost. That is a matter of no small concern when the issue is cost reduction. Second, these arguments emphasize information networks and software packages that can process information to facilitate decisions, which is equivalent to outsourcing the institution's capacity for analysis. Third, the people who make policy on the use of technology in administration should be selected not only for their knowledge of technology and their administrative ability but also because they understand the role of analysis and they can relate information technology to analytical techniques and personnel.

Challenges Facing Research Universities

In Chapter Four, Froomkin focuses on research-intensive universities and the difficult choices that they face. There is an overproduction of doctoral graduates. Universities need to downsize their graduate schools and be selective about the areas in which they will support research so as to maintain quality of effort. This prospect raises several challenges.

First, reducing the scale of graduate enrollment can improve the finances of a university to the extent that it eliminates the need for faculty positions, since tuition alone is not likely to cover both the instructional time and the departmental research time of a faculty member. However, it is not helpful beyond the point at which enrollment no longer permits economical class size.

Second, reducing the breadth of a graduate program by eliminating courses with small enrollments should be pursued only to the extent these are not important from the standpoint of attracting and servicing students in subject areas in which the institution will seek to concentrate.

Third, reducing the extent to which the institution supports basic research that requires expensive facilities may require an institution to balance its ability to attract quality faculty in instructional areas and their likely contribution to knowledge with the extent to which research relies on university funds. Conflict between academic and financial considerations will also be present if basic research is supported partly because of the prospect of lucrative commercial applications (see Nora and Olivas, 1988).

Government research support could be allocated more wisely if all projects were subject to scientific peer group review and the practice of directly earmarking funds that is part of congressional patronage were abandoned. Another question is whether research in a particular field would be more effective if it were concentrated at a single university or at centers at universities that have a particularly strong research faculty in the specialization. Elsewhere (Simpson, 1991), I have argued for the latter position. An allocation of research funds among institutions simply to equalize the largess or to stimulate the local economy is not recommended.

In Chapter Four, Froomkin does not discuss the complicated subject of reimbursement by the federal government for research costs, an area in which an individual institution's expenditures could be reduced. Two issues should be explored: the government's insistence on mandatory cost sharing by the university of a portion of the direct cost of government-sponsored research and the reimbursement for indirect cost. As executive director of a research organization at the University of Chicago in the period after World War II, I found that a government agency was using individual consultant contracts to pick off staff members. To counteract the agency's practice, I negotiated contracts in which support was received for the full range of features of the research environment that were conducive to group and individual productivity: staff professional travel, support for invited scholars, distribution of discussion papers, publication of research monographs, and so forth.

The Council of Governmental Relations and the Association of American Universities (1992) studied reimbursement of indirect cost. Using a sample of twenty-one universities that together accounted for 26 percent of total expenditures for university research, the researchers found that "universities do not receive reimbursement for a substantial fraction of identified costs of research, and therefore are engaged to a significant degree in sharing costs with external sponsors" (1992, p. 4). Despite the fact that we need broader support for the environment that makes research fruitful, we must face the prospect that limitations may be placed on overhead charges (Jaschik, 1993).

Froomkin is skeptical about the prospect that research universities may improve their financial position by sharing in the income generated by applications of their basic research. He identifies four difficulties. First, the academic tradition of open communication makes it difficult for a university to derive financial benefit from its research. Proposed changes in the patent laws may increase that difficulty (Burd, 1992). Second, faculty researchers may utilize university resources up to a point, then continue privately so as to retain the benefits of their research results. Even faculty who have been paid well with the understanding that outside income was to be shared with the university have evaded their responsibility in this way. Third, individual faculty consultant contracts with government or industry may not provide for institutional overhead or for university participation in financial rewards. Fourth, industry may develop research parks and draw upon academic personnel without sharing the resulting proceeds with the university whose staff it employs. In fact, one feature of the information revolution is that scholarly research may no longer depend on a university context. I add a fifth difficulty: There is conflict of interest when faculty members who depend on corporations for salary or research support present themselves as impartial spokespersons.

Universities are under pressure from government agencies to emphasize the potential commercial use of research (Cordes, 1992), and President Clinton's new technology policy calls for close collaboration among universities, labor, and industry (Cordes, 1993). However, the problems encountered become more complex when a university becomes dependent financially on funding from business or becomes a partner in a private business corporation (Bourke and Weissman, 1990; Chaddock, 1992; Blumenstyk, 1993; Wheeler, 1993).

Facilitating Decisions

Chapter Five describes the role of the institutional research office. Bloomfield views that role as one of facilitating the decision process by developing information, identifying and analyzing options, and advancing the forward view. In Chapter Six, Gappa discusses participation in the making of decisions.

Not all practitioners of institutional research will share the view of responsibilities expressed here. Where it is accepted, preparation in the following fields, among others, should be represented within the staff: mathematics, statistical inference and the testing of hypotheses (not simply descriptive statistics), economic theory, and econometrics.

Institutional research personnel can assist in developing what Bloomfield calls a vision statement, which gives a degree of concreteness to the institution's pursuit of its mission in the context of its anticipated internal and external environment. They can also help the campus community to understand the implications for their respective roles and to reach a consensus of support. Since, as Bloomfield points out, that process takes time and since time may be scarce in critical financial situations, an early start is needed.

To a considerable extent, a vision statement is implemented through budget decisions. The most common budget decisions are changes from the prior year and involve some combination of incremental and structural changes in programs.

In reaching a budget decision, various options should be considered. The combination of options that is selected should be the one that analysis shows to represent an allocation of resources that would produce the optimum combination of outputs given the institution's objectives.

Some complications may be noted: A single activity or program can serve several objectives, and a single objective can be served by several programs. Options are interrelated not only by being in competition for inputs (so that benefits foregone are costs), but the processes can interact, and, moreover, the outputs can have effects on one another. Further complications are the nonquantitative nature of certain criteria, the uncertainty attached to alternative scenarios, and the need to take into account the institution's situation if things do not work out.

Although planning-programming-budgeting is not now often employed, it has the virtue of providing a useful framework for the relating of resources to the objectives to be served. However, this virtue can be compromised if objectives are replaced with functions or specific programs (Simpson, 1967, 1985).

Formal cost-benefit analysis may not be warranted—more approximative methods or even an intuitive judgment may suffice—but the decision to forego the use of formal techniques should not result from lack of access to the needed skills.

Participation in Decisions

Gappa points out in Chapter Six that the mission and culture of a college or university influence how it organizes participation in decisions, and she considers some decision models. From my perspective, the essential element in the shared governance model is faculty participation in the formulating and recommending of policy. In the corporate management model, it is the authority of administrators to direct, and in the total quality management model, it is the contribution that teamwork can make to the attainment of a given objective. The challenge facing a college or university is to combine aspects of all three models so as to capitalize on their strengths and minimize their disadvantages, consistent with the values held by participants. With both Chapters Five and Six in mind, institutional research personnel could interpret their role not simply as one of serving the administration's information needs but as one of facilitating the decision process for all participants.

Chapter Six does not address participation by disinterested parties. We already have such participation in the form of visiting accreditation committees, occasional use of outside consultants, and the advisory panels appointed by some departments. Further examples are what I have termed *governance audit* and *optimization review* (Simpson, 1985, 1991). Further, for such matters as retirement packages for university presidents, thoughtful advance comments from observers outside academe are appropriate and useful.

Elsewhere (Simpson, 1993), I have suggested that those in academic life should maintain contact with the public so that the term *ivory tower* comes to mean protected environment within which the mind has full play and not an environment that protects academics from reality. Making it possible for the public to identify with the efforts of higher education is important in building support for increased resources.

References

Albright, M. J., and Graf, D. L. (eds.). *Teaching in the Information Age: The Role of Educational Technology.* New Directions for Teaching and Learning, no. 51. San Francisco: Jossey-Bass, 1992.

Blumenstyk, G. "Colleges Eye More Rigorous Policies to Guard Against Conflicts of Interest." *Chronicle of Higher Education,* Feb. 24, 1993, pp. A29, A31.

Bourke, J., and Weissman, R. "Academics at Risk: The Temptations of Profit." *Academe,* 1990, 76 (5), 15–21.

Burd, S. "Proposed Changes in Patent Laws Would Cripple Universities' Licensing Efforts, Scientists Say." *Chronicle of Higher Education,* Oct. 7, 1992, pp. A21, A25.

Chaddock, G. R. "Industry Becoming the Big Partner on U.S. Campuses." *Los Angeles Times,* Dec. 13, 1992, p. E9.

Collins, J. S., and Hanson, K. H. "Student Financial Aid." In D. M. Greene (ed.), *College and University Business Administration.* (5th ed.) Vol. 3. Washington, D.C.: National Association of College and University Business Officers, 1992.

Cordes, C. "Debate Flares Over Growing Pressures on Academe for Ties with Industry." *Chronicle of Higher Education,* Sept. 16, 1992, pp. A26–A27, A29.

Cordes, C. "Clinton Envisions Strong Federal Role in Developing Commercial Technologies." *Chronicle of Higher Education,* Mar. 3, 1993, pp. A22, A27.

Council on Governmental Relations and Association of American Universities. *Study on the Cost of Research.* Washington, D.C.: Association of American Universities, 1992.

Emery, J. C. (ed.). *Planning for Computing in Higher Education.* EDUCOM Series on Computing and Telecommunications in Higher Education No. 5. Boulder, Colo.: Westview Press, 1980.

Hearn, J. C. "The Teaching Role of Contemporary American Higher Education: Popular Imagery and Organizational Reality." In W. E. Becker and D. R. Lewis (eds.), *The Economics of American Higher Education.* Boston: Kluwer Academic, 1992.

Hefzallah, I. M. (ed.). *The New Learning and Telecommunications Technologies: Their Potential Applications in Education.* Springfield, Ill.: Thomas, 1990.

Jackson, G. A. "Evaluating Learning Technology, Methods, Strategies, and Examples in Higher Education." *Journal of Higher Education,* 1990, 61 (3), 294–311.

Jaschik, S. "Administration Plans Upper Limit on Overhead Charges." *Chronicle of Higher Education*, Feb. 24, 1993, p. A24.

Munshi, K. "The Economics of Telecommunications-Based Distance Learning." *T.H.E. Journal: Technological Horizons in Education*, 1980, 7 (6), 54–57.

Nora, A., and Olivas, M. A. "Faculty Attitudes Toward Industrial Research on Campus." *Research in Higher Education*, 1988, *20* (2), 125–147.

Percival, F., Craig, D., and Buglass, D. *Aspects of Educational Technology.* Vol. 20: *Flexible Learning Systems.* New York: Nichols, 1987.

Simpson, W. B. *Orientation on Program Budgeting.* Los Angeles: Chancellor's Systemwide Task Force on Planning-Programming-Budgeting, California State Colleges, 1967.

Simpson, W. B. "Revitalizing the Role of Values and Objectives in Institutions of Higher Education: Difficulties Encountered and the Possible Contribution of External Evaluation." *Higher Education*, 1985, *14*, 535–551.

Simpson, W. B. "Income-Contingent Student Loans: Context, Potential, and Limits." *Higher Education*, 1987, *16*, 699–721.

Simpson, W. B. "Review of L. E. Gladieux (ed.), *Radical Reform or Incremental Change? Student Loan Policy Alternatives for the Federal Government.*" *Academe*, 1989, 75 (6), 56.

Simpson, W. B. *Cost Containment for Higher Education: Strategies for Public Policy and Institutional Administration.* New York: Praeger, 1991.

Simpson, W. B. "Higher Education's Role in a New Beginning." *Academe*, 1993, *79* (1), 17–21.

Simpson, W. B., and Mendelson, M. "Student Loans: A Moderate Proposal." *Academe*, 1986, 72 (6), 19–21.

Snowden, B. L., and Daniel, J. S. "The Economics and Management of Small Post-Secondary Distance Education Systems." *Distance Education*, 1980, *1* (1), 68–91.

Wheeler, D. L. "A Case Study: One Scientist's Ties to a Biotechnology Company." *Chronicle of Higher Education*, Feb. 24, 1993, pp. A29, A30.

WILLIAM B. SIMPSON is emeritus professor of economics at California State University, Los Angeles, and formerly was managing editor and coeditor of Econometrica *and executive director of the Cowles Commission for Research in Economics at the University of Chicago.*

INDEX

Tuition, 1 2, 7, 8, 13, 17 18, 51, 52 53, 67 68, 86, 89. *See also* Student financial aid

Ulbrich, H. H., 28, 29
U.S. Department of Education, 5, 15
University of California, 50, 55
University of Chicago, 57, 89
University of Illinois, Urbana-Champaign, 36 37
University of Michigan, 51

Vinea, V., 42, 45
Vision statements, 61 63, 90 91
Volkwein, J. F., 20, 29, 63, 64

Wagener, U., 73, 83
Weissman, R., 90, 92
Wergin, J. F., 68, 71
West, T. W., 41, 45
Wheeler, D. L., 90, 93
Winter, D. G., 27, 29
Wolfle, D., 49, 58
Wolvin, A. D., 74, 83

Yale University, 73

Zammuto, R. F., 63, 71
Zemsky, R., 7, 14, 23, 29

Ordering Information

NEW DIRECTIONS FOR INSTITUTIONAL RESEARCH is a series of paperback books that provides planners and administrators in all types of academic institutions with guidelines in such areas as resource coordination, information analysis, program evaluation, and institutional management. Books in the series are published quarterly in Spring, Summer, Fall, and Winter and are available for purchase by subscription as well as by single copy.

SUBSCRIPTIONS for 1993 cost $47.00 for individuals (a savings of 25 percent over single-copy prices) and $62.00 for institutions, agencies, and libraries. Please do not send institutional checks for personal subscriptions. Standing orders are accepted.

SINGLE COPIES cost $15.95 when payment accompanies order. (California, New Jersey, New York, and Washington, D.C., residents please include appropriate sales tax.) Billed orders will be charged postage and handling.

DISCOUNTS FOR QUANTITY ORDERS are available. Please write to the address below for information.

ALL ORDERS must include either the name of an individual or an official purchase order number. Please submit your order as follows:
    Subscriptions: specify series and year subscription is to begin
    Single copies: include individual title code (such as IR78)

MAIL ALL U.S. ORDERS TO:
    Jossey-Bass Publishers
    350 Sansome Street
    San Francisco, CA 94104-1342

FOR SINGLE-COPY SALES OUTSIDE OF THE UNITED STATES CONTACT:
    Maxwell Macmillan International Publishing Group
    866 Third Avenue
    New York, NY 10022-6221

FOR SUBSCRIPTION SALES OUTSIDE OF THE UNITED STATES, contact
    any international subscription agency, or Jossey-Bass directly.

Statement of Ownership, Management and Circulation
(Required by 39 U.S.C. 3685)

#82310
e-p.106

1A. Title of Publication	1B. PUBLICATION NO. *(ISSN)*	2. Date of Filing
NEW DIRECTIONS FOR INSTITUTIONAL RESEARCH	0 2 7 1 0 5 7 9	12/13/93

3. Frequency of Issue	3A. No. of Issues Published Annually	3B. Annual Subscription Price
Quarterly	Four (4)	$47.00(personal) $62.00(institutional

4. Complete Mailing Address of Known Office of Publication *(Street, City, County, State and ZIP+4 Code) (Not printers)*

350 Sansome Street, San Francisco, CA 94104-1342 (San Francisco County)

5. Complete Mailing Address of the Headquarters of General Business Offices of the Publisher *(Not printer)*

(above address)

6. Full Names and Complete Mailing Address of Publisher, Editor, and Managing Editor *(This item MUST NOT be blank)*

Publisher *(Name and Complete Mailing Address)*

Jossey-Bass Inc., Publishers (above address)

Editor *(Name and Complete Mailing Address)*

Patrick T. Terenzini, Ctr for the Study of Higher Educ, Pennsylvania State Univ 403 S Allen Street, Suite 104, University Park, PA 16801-5202

Managing Editor *(Name and Complete Mailing Address)*

Lynn D. Luckow, President, Jossey-Bass Inc., Publishers (address above)

7. Owner *(If owned by a corporation, its name and address must be stated and also immediately thereunder the names and addresses of stockholders owning or holding 1 percent or more of total amount of stock. If not owned by a corporation, the names and addresses of the individual owners must be given. If owned by a partnership or other unincorporated firm, its name and address, as well as that of each individual must be given. If the publication is published by a nonprofit organization, its name and address must be stated.) (Item must be completed.)*

Full Name	Complete Mailing Address
Macmillan, Inc.	55 Railroad Avenue Greenwich, CT 06830-6378

8. Known Bondholders, Mortgagees, and Other Security Holders Owning or Holding 1 Percent or More of Total Amount of Bonds, Mortgages or Other Securities *(If there are none, so state)*

Full Name	Complete Mailing Address
same as above	same as above

9. For Completion by Nonprofit Organizations Authorized To Mail at Special Rates *(DMM Section 424.12 only)*
The purpose, function, and nonprofit status of this organization and the exempt status for Federal income tax purposes *(Check one)*

(1) ☐ Has Not Changed During Preceding 12 Months	(2) ☐ Has Changed During Preceding 12 Months	*(If changed, publisher must submit explanation of change with this statement.)*

10.	Extent and Nature of Circulation *(See instructions on reverse side)*	Average No. Copies Each Issue During Preceding 12 Months	Actual No. Copies of Single Issue Published Nearest to Filing Date
A.	Total No. Copies *(Net Press Run)*	2,010	2,150
B.	Paid and/or Requested Circulation 1. Sales through dealers and carriers, street vendors and counter sales	451	512
	2. Mail Subscription *(Paid and/or requested)*	762	716
C.	Total Paid and/or Requested Circulation *(Sum of 10B1 and 10B2)*	1,213	1,228
D.	Free Distribution by Mail, Carrier or Other Means Samples, Complimentary, and Other Free Copies	66	66
E.	Total Distribution *(Sum of C and D)*	1,279	1,294
F.	Copies Not Distributed 1. Office use, left over, unaccounted, spoiled after printing	731	856
	2. Return from News Agents	0	0
G.	TOTAL *(Sum of E, F1 and 2—should equal net press run shown in A)*	2,010	2,150

11. I certify that the statements made by me above are correct and complete	Signature and Title of Editor, Publisher, Business Manager, or Owner	Larry Ishii Vice President

PS Form 3526, January 1991